The Little Book of
Cacti &
Succulents

RHS The Little Book of Cacti and Succulents

Author: Sophie Collins

First published in Great Britain in 2022 by Mitchell Beazley, a division of
Octopus Publishing Group Ltd
Carmelite House, 50 Victoria Embankment, London EC4Y 0DZ
www.octopusbooks.co.uk
An Hachette UK Company
www.hachette.co.uk

Published in association with the Royal Horticultural Society

ISBN: 978-1-78472-834-2

A CIP record of this book is available from the British Library

Printed and bound in China

Conceived, designed and produced by The Bright Press
an imprint of The Quarto Group
The Old Brewery, 6 Blundell Street,
London N7 9BH, United Kingdom
T (0) 20 7700 6700
www.Quarto.com

Publisher: James Evans
Art Director: James Lawrence
Editorial Director: Isheeta Mustafi
Managing Editor: Jacqui Sayers
Project Editor: Kathleen Steeden
Design: Lindsey Johns
Illustrations: John Woodcock, Ellis Rose

Mitchell Beazley Publisher: Alison Starling
RHS Publisher: Rae Spencer-Jones
RHS Consultant Editor: Simon Maughan
RHS Head of Editorial: Tom Howard

FSC — MIX — Paper from responsible sources — FSC® C016973

The Royal Horticultural Society is the UK's leading gardening charity dedicated to advancing
horticulture and promoting good gardening. Its charitable work includes providing expert advice
and information, training the next generation of gardeners, creating hands-on opportunities for
children to grow plants and conducting research into plants, pests and environmental issues
affecting gardeners.

For more information visit www.rhs.org.uk or call 0845 130 4646.

The Little Book of
Cacti &
Succulents

A COMPLETE GUIDE TO CHOOSING,
GROWING AND DISPLAYING

SOPHIE COLLINS

CONTENTS

INTRODUCTION

If you're new to growing cacti and succulents, you might think that those plus points most often claimed for them – that they're good for beginners and easy to keep – sound a bit dull. And that's a pity, because this huge and varied group of plants isn't just easygoing, it also includes species with masses of visual appeal, many of which will fit beautifully into pretty much any corner of your living space.

Succulents come in shapes ranging from architectural globes and columns to exquisitely intricate rosette structures, and fountain-like waterfalls of stems that are perfectly suited to hanging containers. Colour-wise, they're varied too; some plants in maroon-reds and oranges; others covering a gamut of greens, from lime to viridian; and still others in subtle neutrals and greys. Last but by no means least, you'll find succulents in textures that would do credit to a fashionable paint range, with 'finishes' from matt to glossy, soft to spiny and shiny to furry – or even powdery.

Put all these aspects together and they make cacti and succulents some of the most varied and attractive plants you can grow, so it's no wonder that they've become so popular over the last few years. As houseplants they're infinitely adaptable, whether your space is large or small. You can start a succulent table on a balcony or patio with the hardier types, choose a single big column cactus for a corner of your sitting room and pick humidity-friendly rainforest species to add lushness to your bathroom.

As you learn more about the different groups, you'll be able to choose the right plants for projects ranging from table terrariums to windows framed with hanging baskets or tiny living fridge magnets in pots. *The Little Book of Cacti & Succulents* will get you started, offering all the practical information you need to begin a collection and keep it in good order, and will act as a springboard for your creativity when it comes to decorating with plants, both indoors and out.

Left You can mix different succulent species in the same container to make the most of the variety of colours and textures, but check that your chosen species share the same care needs before potting them up together.

HOW TO USE THIS BOOK

Whatever your pedigree as a gardener – and whatever your level of experience with houseplants – the five chapters in this book offer a complete guide to buying and growing succulents. You'll find it succinct, straightforward and inspirational.

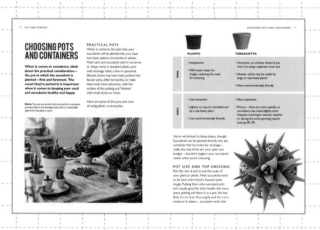

CHAPTER 1

An introduction to the succulent family, looking at key characteristics and the basics you need to know – from pot sizes to potting soil mixes – to grow succulents successfully.

CHAPTER 2

Where to buy your plants – online or in person – and how to look after your new collection. What succulents need to thrive, in terms of light, warmth and water, plus an explanation of dormancy (and why it can be a good, or even a necessary thing for your plants).

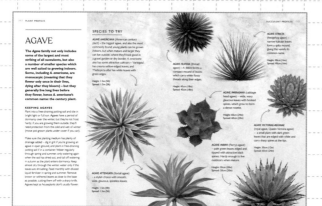

CHAPTER 3

How to show off your plants at their best – how to group and curate them, with copious ideas for arrangements that will fit pretty much any space, indoors or out. Including some step-by-step projects to stimulate your own creativity.

CHAPTER 4

Plant profiles, enabling you to shop around for the ideal species to suit your space. There's a mix here of single plants and group spreads – the latter takes a succinct look across a whole plant family that's particularly suited to succulent-growing novices.

CHAPTER 5

A straightforward, easy-to-follow guide to extending your plant collection economically – looking at growing from seed, and at propagating from leaves or cuttings.

CHAPTER ONE

Getting Started

The sheer number of different succulents available can make it hard for you to know where to begin. This chapter offers a succinct introduction to the group – and explains, too, why all cacti are succulents, but not all succulents are cacti – followed by sections that cover what you need to know about containers, potting soil and the very simple equipment you'll need to keep your new plants happy.

As well as these basics, it takes a first look at some of the decorative effects that you can achieve, simply by matching a plant and its container to a situation, with plenty of images to start you thinking about what might look good in your own home. Attractive shelf arrangements or table centrepieces including plants will liven up indoor spaces, while more ambitious ideas, such as a trio of hanging baskets made from simple wire vegetable storage hangers, can be surprisingly easy to achieve.

The chapter rounds off with a useful overview of which succulents will cope in an outdoor environment, on a terrace, balcony or patio, and which will be better off living a more sheltered life indoors.

WHAT ARE CACTI AND SUCCULENTS?

'Cacti and succulents' is often used as a catchall term to describe a huge range of plants, but what actually defines them? And why are the two words always linked together? Here are some answers to the questions most frequently asked by gardeners new to the group.

DESERT DWELLERS

Rather than being a neat taxonomic group, 'succulents' refers to a loose collection of species, incorporating around 60 different plant families, bound together by shared characteristics. The majority of succulents originate in dry habitats, deserts and semi-deserts, where there is a lot of light and heat; thin, free-draining soil; and not much water (there are a few forest-dwelling exceptions to the rule, which have slightly different habits and needs).

In order to survive such tough, arid conditions, succulents have developed the capacity to store water and nutrients in their swollen stems and leaves. This provides them with an effective defence against drought and also gives them their highly recognizable, rather fleshy appearance. In addition, most have a thick, waxy coating that minimizes water loss.

WHAT MAKES A SUCCULENT A CACTUS?

All succulents have evolved to store water in their stems and leaves, sometimes in one or the other, sometimes in both, so they cope unusually well without regular water – they're the camels of the horticultural world.

Cacti, as a subgroup, have modifications of their own. Some are unique to them, while others are found more commonly in cacti than other succulents.

SUCCULENTS	CACTI
• Come from all over the world	• Are native only to the Americas
• Have swollen stems and leaves or spikes	• Generally have swollen stems, but often also spikes which are highly modified leaves
• Don't have areoles – raised bumps on the stem surface from which spines and flowers emerge	• Have areoles

Thick, waxy skin surface minimizes water loss

Leaf

Stem

Spikes, actually modified leaves, discourage grazing animals

Areole

Stem

MAKING IT WORK

Succulents also have fewer stomates – the pore-like structures which allow the exchange of gases in photosynthesis – than most other plants, and they have developed a modified form of the key process of photosynthesis. Most plants open their stomates in the daytime to collect carbon dioxide, but if succulents did this in high daytime temperatures, they'd lose too much water; instead, they open their comparatively few stomates at night when the desert temperatures drop, then store the carbon dioxide they collect to use for photosynthesis the following day. This adjustment has the tongue-tripping name of crassulacean acid metabolism, CAM for short, and it's believed to be a factor in the comparatively slow growth and long lives of many succulents.

LIVING IN THE FORESTS

The exceptions to the desert dwellers mentioned above are the epiphytic cacti, succulents that live at high altitude, in the forests of Central and South America. Epiphytes live on the trees, rooting themselves in the debris that accumulates between branches. Popular and widely available examples include the Christmas and Easter cacti (*Shlumbergera* and *Hatiora* respectively). This group have different needs from those of the desert succulents – they can cope with more humidity and lower levels of light – and different habits when it comes to their pattern of growth and dormancy (see pp.38–39).

SLOW GROWERS

In general, succulents aren't quick to put on growth, although many make up for it by living long lives. Some grow faster than others, though, so if you're the impatient type, you may want to make sure that you have some hares as well as tortoises in your collection.

Left As this Easter cactus (*Hatiora gaertneri*) shows, some succulents are spectacular when in flower.

FIVE SPEEDY SPECIES TO TRY

All five of these are good-looking plants with structural interest – which, given favourable conditions, are also gratifyingly quick to put on new growth. You'll find more detailed descriptions in the plant directory in Chapter 4.

Purple houseleek (*Aeonium arboreum*)
In its native Madagascar, this plant becomes a substantial shrub, growing up to 2m (6ft 6in) tall. It may not reach these dizzy heights in your living room, but it's still a plant to be reckoned with.

Money plant, jade plant (*Crassula ovata*)
A popular classic, believed to bring luck, this succulent can easily put on as much as 25cm (10in) in a year.

Mexican snow ball (*Echeveria elegans*)
One of the bigger echeveria species, the intricate rosette of this plant will quickly develop a spread of around 33cm (12in).

Blue jelly bean plant (*Sedum pachyphyllum*) The tactile clusters of 'jelly beans' that give the plant its name quickly become long, drooping stems.

String of pearls, string of beads (*Curio rowleyanus* syn. *Senecio rowleyanus*) Just a few of the 'beads' will grow into long strings well within a year.

TOOLS AND EQUIPMENT

You don't need many tools to care for succulents, and you'll probably find that you have some of what you do need already. Some things can also be improvised. A few specifics, though, will be useful to help you keep your plants well cared-for, dust-free and looking their best.

CACTUS GLOVES You can work bare-handed or use regular gardening gloves, but if you become enthusiastic about the spikier members of the group, it may be worth investing in a pair of cactus gloves. They're usually made from stretchy fabric with pads to protect your palms and fingers, made from a special material that is completely spine-proof. A cactus collar (see box, right) is a useful improvised way to move spiky plants around, too.

SMALL TROWEL OR SPOON An 'indoor' or small trowel is handy for potting plants up or mixing different potting mediums, particularly if you're working indoors in a limited space. Alternatively, you can improvise with a metal tablespoon, which will do most jobs equally well.

SPRAY BOTTLE Useful for misting plants to give additional humidity for those that appreciate it, and for dampening leaves before cleaning.

INDOOR WATERING CAN A small watering can with a narrow spout, which gives you control over the amount of water you're pouring – this is important when many cacti and succulents don't appreciate being saturated.

PRUNING SHEARS, SHARP-BLADED KNIFE OR SCISSORS To trim or lightly prune plants to keep them neat. A sharp-bladed knife is often also the cleanest way to take a leaf or stem for a cutting.

MAKE A CACTUS COLLAR

You can use a piece of plastic bubble wrap to help you handle prickly plants, but there's a greener way of doing it that's just as effective.

Take two sheets of newspaper, line them up so the edges match and concertina-fold them along the long edges until you've made a strip around 10cm (4in) wide, then flatten. Holding the strip's ends, you can use this as a collar around spiny plants when you're handling them, to avoid getting spiked.

SMALL PAINTBRUSHES A narrow decorator's paintbrush and an artist's brush can both be used for brushing off loose soil after repotting, for dealing with pests or for dusting plants.

THERMOMETER This is useful to check on certain spots – a windowsill in full summer sun, for example, may prove too hot for some plants in your collection.

CHOOSING POTS AND CONTAINERS

When it comes to containers, think about the practical consideration – the pot in which the succulent is planted – first and foremost. The vessel they're potted in is important when it comes to keeping your cacti and succulents healthy and happy.

Below You can use pretty much any pot for a succulent provided that it has drainage holes and is a reasonably tight fit for the plant's roots.

PRACTICAL POTS

When it comes to the pots that your succulents will be planted into, you have two basic options: terracotta or plastic. Most cacti and succulents sold in nurseries or shops come in standard plastic pots with drainage holes; a few in upmarket lifestyle stores may have been potted into fancier pots, often terracotta, to make them look more attractive, with the surface of the potting soil 'finished' with small stones or moss.

Here are some of the pros and cons of using plastic vs terracotta.

PLASTIC

TERRACOTTA

	PLASTIC	TERRACOTTA
PROS	• Inexpensive • Will retain water for longer, reducing the need for watering	• Attractive, so a better choice if you won't be using a separate outer pot • Heavier, which may be useful for large or top-heavy plants • More environmentally friendly
CONS	• Less attractive • Lighter, so may be overbalanced by a top-heavy plant • Less environmentally friendly	• More expensive • Porous – dries out more quickly, so succulents may need slightly more frequent watering in warmer weather or during the active growing season (see pp.38–39)

You're not limited to these basics, though. Succulents can be planted directly into any container that has holes for drainage – really, the only limits are your taste and budget – but don't neglect your succulents' needs when you're choosing.

POT SIZE AND TOP DRESSING

Pick the size of pot to suit the scale of your plant or plants. Most succulents tend to do best when they're housed quite snugly. Putting them into oversized pots isn't usually good for their health: the more spare potting soil there is in a pot, the less likely it is to drain thoroughly and the more moisture it retains – succulent roots that

stay damp are prone to rot. When you're matching succulent to container, allow the same depth as width in the pot for the plant's roots.

Once potted, adding top dressing around the succulent will also help to keep it healthy. A layer of small pebbles or gravel on top of the soil ensures that the plant doesn't rest directly against damp soil after watering and acts as another guard against rot. Top dressing can also look decorative: there are plenty of different textures and colours of pebbles and gravel available. Beachcombed sea glass or coloured glass pebbles are other options.

Below A succulent collection arranged in mismatched and varied containers can look just as striking as a pristine line-up housed in matching pastel or monochrome pots.

DECORATIVE POTS AND SLEEVES

When you've made sure your plant is happily housed, it's time to consider how you want it to look. Simple terracotta pots can look great on their own, but if you want a specific style, you can put the succulent, pot and all, into an outer display container (professional growers call these 'sleeves'). This doesn't need drainage holes, and provided that it's not so deep that it compromises the amount of light that reaches the lower part of the plant, it can be pretty much any style or shape you like. You do need to make sure that, after watering, any drained water is tipped out of the display container, so that the inner pot isn't sitting in a puddle.

TERRARIUMS

For such a popular feature, terrariums raise a surprising amount of controversy – for every fan of the way that they look, there's a gardener worrying about their drawbacks when it comes to the actual needs of plants. Closed terrariums can have a lot of practical disadvantages – they limit air circulation, which can mean that there's too much humidity for their occupants, and they can also get too hot, even for heat-loving succulents. They don't tend to drain well, even with carefully designed 'drainage layers'.

If you like the look of terrariums, some designs will get you the style without compromising your plants' health. Look for glass globes with openings in the side – these are available with flat bases so they can sit on a surface, or with hanging loops so that you can suspend them. They can still get hot, but the opening ensures that the humidity build-up is limited.

HANGING BASKETS AND CONTAINERS

Hanging baskets have some advantages for succulents – air circulates around them easily and provided that they're planted up with the right medium, they have excellent drainage. Of course, they're also one of the best ways to show off those species that trail and sprawl, and there are plenty of suitable cacti and succulents to choose from.

FIND THE RIGHT SPACE

Think about where you're going to hang a basket or container, and what it's going to hang from, before you buy one or plant it up. If you do it the other way round, you may end up with a beautifully planned and arranged container and then find there's no secure place to fit a hook to hang it on. As well as the safety element – no one wants a basket landing on their head – there's also the question of how much direct light and warmth the situation offers. The forest cacti groups usually do better in indirect light, and can also cope with more humidity, a combination which means that they're often a popular choice for bathrooms – while many other succulents will be happy with direct sun, so pick your species according to your situation. Outside, good spots for a hanging basket may be in the shelter of a building's eaves, or hung over a balcony, either of which will shield the basket from heavy rain and offer some protection in colder weather.

WHICH CONTAINER?

Hanging baskets are most often made from plastic, woven fibre or wire. Choose one without a ready-fitted plastic lining (or you can strip the liner out); if you leave it in, the plastic is liable to keep the contents from draining properly. The best options for lining are coir, jute (rough woven fabric) or moss. A metal basket lined with moss or coir is probably the most immediately attractive option, although it's unlikely to be the cheapest (and if you need to go for a more economic choice, don't forget that a basket which might not look so appealing·at first glance won't be nearly as noticeable when it's lined and has been planted up).

Opposite Apart from the conventional hanging basket, there are plenty of more offbeat options for hanging plants. Almost anything can work provided there's enough drainage to ensure the plants aren't left sitting in wet potting soil.

USING LINERS

If you opt to use moss to line a basket, it's a more environmentally friendly choice either to collect it yourself from a mossy lawn (your own or a friend's) or to find a local supplier who collects it sustainably, rather than to buy packs of sphagnum peat moss from a nursery. Soak a handful of moss in water, then squeeze it out with your hands and press the damp moss against the inside of the basket. Repeat until the basket is fully lined, then leave the moss to dry out; as it dries, it will shape itself to the basket. Coir, a fibrous material derived from coconuts, is another comparatively green option. It is also extremely straightforward to use – it's sold in the form of readymade liners in a variety of sizes; just fit the appropriate one straight into the basket. Jute comes as flat fabric; dampen it, fit it into the basket, then trim the material to neaten it around the top edge.

SIDE PLANTING

Side planting simply means adding plants at the sides of the basket rather than filling it entirely from the top. It can give a basket more visual impact when it's hanging, but you do need to cut holes in either a coir or jute liner to push the plants through, so you'll need to plan where you're going to place a plant or plants at the sides before you add your potting soil. (If you've lined with moss, you can gently pull some out until you've made a hole the right size for your plant.)

POTTING UP

Use the same medium in a hanging basket
as you would in a pot, but allow around a
third perlite to two-thirds potting soil, to
make the mixture, and therefore the
finished basket, lighter (see pp.26–7).
Choose plants with complementary needs
if you're mixing species, and place your
plant or plants in the basket as you fill it,
rather than putting in the potting soil and
then digging out holes for the plants, which
tends to compact the soil as you dig.

HANGING POTS

Macrame holders enclosing regular pots
or sometimes baskets have been stalwarts
for houseplants since the 1970s and show
no signs of losing their appeal – if anything,
they've enjoyed a resurgence in popularity
over the last few years. If you like the look,
they're highly adaptable: the knotted
structure makes them stretchy, so they
can be adjusted to fit different pot sizes
or shapes.

LOOKING UP

In terms of day-to-day care,
hanging containers, whether pots
or baskets, need the same attention
– watering, occasional feeding and
tidying/pruning – as their counterparts
on the ground. The main risk to their
wellbeing is that, sitting above your
immediate eyeline, they may
get forgotten.

POTTING SOIL FOR SUCCULENTS

When it comes to potting soil, the main point to remember is that cacti and succulents must have good drainage to thrive. You can buy a commercial specialist cactus potting soil for your plants, but it's relatively expensive, and it's easy enough to mix up your own.

MIXING YOUR OWN

To make your own mixture, you'll need a plastic mixing bowl, a trowel or scoop to measure with, a bag of regular multipurpose peat-free potting compost and a bag of horticultural grit, all of which can be bought at any garden centre or plant nursery. Simply measure out two scoops of compost to one of grit and stir the two together thoroughly before using the mix like any other potting medium.

Below Mix your potting compost and grit or perlite together thoroughly before filling your pots, to ensure even drainage once your succulents are planted up.

USING PERLITE

Perlite is a mineral material that weighs very little. It's white, and looks a bit like polystyrene granules, but it's actually produced by heating volcanic glass until it 'pops' into small porous balls. It is available in bags from garden centres and, mixed in with compost either with or instead of grit, it makes a lighter mixture with improved aeration which drains even more freely (it's often included in the commercial specialist potting soil).

It comes in useful when the weight of the planting medium matters (when you're planting up succulents in hanging baskets, for example). You can also use it to make a mix that will suit some desert species, such as *Lithops* (see p.123), which originate in extremely arid environments and will appreciate the enhanced drainage and aeration to their roots. Perlite can be dusty and it's not good for you to breathe it in, so wear a mask when you're using it. To add it to your planting mix, add one scoop of perlite to the two scoops compost/one scoop grit formula given above and ensure all three are mixed together thoroughly.

PLAYING WITH PROPORTIONS
You can vary the proportions of perlite and horticultural grit used in your soil mixtures – if the end mixture needs to be light, cut down on the grit and add more perlite.

INDOORS OR OUTDOORS?

Despite succulents holding a well-earned place as top-ranking houseplants, quite a lot of the hardier species can cope with life outdoors, at least in the warmer months (see pp.76–79). And a few, including sempervivums, sedums and some species of aeoniums and aloes will usually, though not invariably, survive outside year-round provided that they're given some shelter.

HARDY SPECIMENS

Succulents will always need very good drainage, so are unlikely to thrive in a damp border, say, and leaving any outside year-round inevitably carries a degree of risk. The best middle path is probably to keep your plants in containers and to bring them in to shelter (either indoors, into a greenhouse if you're lucky enough to have one, or under cover on a porch or balcony) when autumn comes, and the weather starts to get colder and wetter. When temperatures fall below 5°C (41°F) most succulents will need protection, although damp is more of a threat than dry, cold weather.

THE BEST OF BOTH WORLDS

Always check the specific details of a valued plant before you decide it can cope outside. If it's going to live outdoors, for the summer at least, follow the tips in the box opposite to make its transition as easy as possible.

If you like arranging and then rearranging your containers and trying out different effects, then the opportunity to make a new display outside in summer and trying out alternative looks indoors in winter will be one of the enjoyable pluses of a cactus and succulent collection.

Opposite An appealingly arranged planter of succulents can act as a focal point outdoors in summer and be brought back indoors over the winter.

KEEPING SUCCULENTS OUTSIDE

Raise containers Using pot feet or stones, raise your containers off the ground. This both protects your plants from contact with the ground and ensures that any additional water drains away.

Add a dry top layer Add a generous layer of small stones or gravel as a top dressing on pots, around the plant stem. This ensures that lower stems or leaves stay clear of the damp surface of the soil.

Keep your plants tidy Pick up any dropped leaves and remove any damaged or dead stems or leaves – if you leave them, they'll encourage damp, which may in turn cause rot.

Wrap up warm When temperatures fall to 5°C (41°F) or lower, consider wrapping valued plants lightly in garden fleece overnight. Don't wrap them too closely; they'll still need room to breathe.

CHAPTER TWO

Caring For Your Collection

The 'thrives on benign neglect' label is one that gets attached to cacti and succulents rather too often. While it's true that they aren't generally hard to care for, like any other plants, they'll grow best when they're treated the way that they like. This chapter will help to turn you from someone who owns a few succulents into an indoor gardener who feels confident enough to make a healthy, lush indoor jungle of their own.

We start by looking at where you get your succulents and the pros and cons of buying in person versus buying online. There's a succinct guide to their everyday care with suggestions for a few can't-fail species if you're a complete beginner. It includes answers to the questions you have about watering and feeding, and takes you through the natural growth and dormancy cycle of succulents — important when it comes to giving your plants an annual rest, especially if you'd like them to flower in the following season. Last but not least, there's a troubleshooting section that looks at some common problems, from sun-scorch to mealybugs, and tells you how to beat them.

CHOOSING CACTI AND SUCCULENTS

What originally attracted you to succulents? Were you seduced by their sculptural shapes or extraordinary textures, or did you see images of a particularly impressive succulent collection and decide that something like that would look great at home? Whether you want a few impressive statement plants or you're aiming for a jungle effect, you need to know where you're going to get the ingredients. It's best, too, to look at how much care individual species may need – and at how they'll fit into your own space – before you buy.

BUYING SUCCULENTS

Most succulents will come from one of four kinds of retailers: you can buy them in person from a general nursery, a specialist grower, or a lifestyle store, or order them from stores or nurseries online. When you're starting a collection, it's best to visit in person if possible: not only does it give you the chance to have a good look at the plants available and pick and choose between them, but you can also ask questions before you buy.

BUYING IN PERSON

A local non-specialist plant nursery is likely to have at least a small choice of popular succulent groups, such as aeoniums and echeverias, plus any extras you may need, such as pots, baskets, specialist potting soil and perlite or horticultural grit. Succulents and cacti have become popular in lifestyle stores over the last decade, too, where they tend to be marketed as part of an appealing home 'look' and are often sold in interiors-ready pots or containers – which look great but may add a premium to the price.

Specialist growers or nurseries will have a wider choice of more unusual species, but may be more expensive, and will often sell larger, more mature plants, including some that may also need more looking after. If you're new to succulents they may not be your first port of call, but as your familiarity with the group grows, a specialist nursery is great for a visit. Not only will you get the chance to look at some wonderful, aspirational plants, but also the enthusiasts who sell them will have lots of knowledge and will usually be keen to share it.

Below and opposite Visiting a nursery in person won't necessarily offer you more species to choose between, but it will give you the opportunity to 'meet' different plants before making your choice.

BUYING ONLINE

Although you won't be able to check individual plants, buying online has its own advantages. First, you'll find a huge choice of sellers and species. Second, many sites offer a lot of free information as well as stock; you can spend a while browsing at a time that suits you. Take your time; most species will usually be available from a lot of different sources. Make the same checks for the needs of a particular species as you would if you were buying from a nursery and asking the seller in person.

Below If you're new to growing succulents, look out for mix-and-match special offers on small groups of plants: these give you the opportunity to try out several different species at once.

A couple of specific points about buying online. Check out the dimensions, both height and spread, of the plant that's being sold – sometimes what seems to be a bargain price may be for a specimen that's smaller than it looks in the picture. Look at the reviews for the store's packaging, too. How carefully a plant is packed and posted is important, as it reflects the state in which you'll receive it.

FINDING BARGAINS

Both nurseries and online sellers may offer some special deals. This can include 'bargain' trays of different types of small succulents, or two-for-one type offers on popular species. These are always worth a look – they can be a good, economical way to introduce you to different species to see if you like them. Succulents that are being sold off as the last of some old stock, though, may not offer equivalent value. Don't take a sick plant home unless you're a natural at horticultural nursing.

ALWAYS QUARANTINE

Whatever its source, when you bring a new plant home, keep it away from the rest of your collection for a couple of weeks, and check it over once a week during this time. This will ensure that you don't accidentally introduce any problems, such as pests, to your other plants.

Aeonium

FIVE GROUPS FOR NOVICES

Most species in these groups are good
starter plants; each group covers plenty
of easily available and inexpensive options.

Aloe

Aeoniums With rosettes that grow flat
to the ground or are carried at the end of
long stems, aeoniums come in colours that
range from deepest purple to palest green.

Aloes These are spiky plants, also with
a rosette structure. They vary in size;
the best known, *Aloe vera*, can reach
60cm (2ft) as a houseplant.

Echeveria

Echeverias The well-known 'hen and
chicks' group, these plants often produce
many offspring from a single 'parent', giving
you free baby plants as a bonus.

Mammillarias Globe-shaped or
columnar, a varied group of small 'typical'
cacti, with lots of intriguing textures, many
spiny and some 'woolly' or hairy, too.

Mammillaria

Sedums Includes both upright forms and
trailers, with shiny, fleshy leaves. Many are
hardy enough to grow outdoors.

Sedum

PLANTS AT HOME

If succulents are a new enthusiasm, check out the space you have at home that can be used to indulge it. What space have you got – a sunny kitchen windowsill? Space above it, which would fit a hanging basket or two? A coffee table that would look good with an arrangement of smaller plants? Think in terms of where plants will fit in and which plants will like a particular situation.

Below Check that any small succulents you plan to display as a group have broadly the same light needs and preferred temperature range.

LIGHT AND HEAT

Bear in mind that you may have to move plants around to give them the right amount of light and warmth at different times of year. All desert succulents need plenty of sun, but a very hot windowsill at the height of summer may actually scorch a plant, while the same spot may be just right in winter when sunlight is in much shorter supply. Avoid placing plants directly next to radiators: the solid, one-way heat is likely to shrivel them. Tropical cacti are happier in filtered or indirect light, so will be fine behind a slatted window shade, or hung to one side of a window, where strong light doesn't hit them straight on, but they don't like being kept in full shade.

STEAMY SITUATIONS

Most succulents prefer not to live in a bathroom or right by a kitchen sink. Both spots will vary in temperature and bathing, showering and washing-up will all create an atmosphere of steamy humidity that won't be to their taste. Epiphytic cacti are the obvious choice here; they'll be happy with a degree of humidity, especially if they can also be placed out of direct sunlight.

Below Watch out for unfortunate encounters between pets and plants. If you can't keep the plant out of reach of a high-climbing cat, block it off safely on a shelf using books or other objects.

STAY SAFE

When you're arranging your plants, bear in mind that many succulents are toxic if eaten, so they should be kept out of the way of small children and curious pets, whether they are resident or just visiting. Watch out, too, for the spikier cacti – they need to be placed in a spot where they won't scratch people passing, or snag on their clothing.

A YEAR IN THE LIFE

Most succulents alternate periods of active growth with periods of dormancy, times when their growth and the rate at which they photosynthesize slow right down. In their natural habitats, growth and dormancy periods are decided by the local climate, and they will enter dormancy when the seasonal levels of light and warmth drop. When they're kept as indoor plants, though, if the amount of warmth and light around them doesn't vary much, some succulents may not undergo dormancy at all.

A dormant period is good for succulents: it gives them an annual rest and, if they are going to flower (some species don't when kept as houseplants), they will do so in the season following dormancy.

ENCOURAGING DORMANCY

With the exception of the epiphytic cacti (see box opposite), most succulents would naturally have their dormant period over the winter months. You can encourage dormancy by tailing off watering and feeding as autumn moves into winter, and by keeping plants at a slightly lower temperature. Make sure, though, that your succulents continue to get plenty of daylight, and sun when it's available, and keep them away from any particularly draughty spots.

Only the tougher succulents – such as some sedums, for example – will cope with overwintering outdoors. If plants are going to stay outside, make sure that they are appropriately sheltered from the damp, and wrap them in horticultural fleece if temperatures fall sharply and there's any chance of frost.

Check Chapter 4 (see pp.74–127) for plants' individual profiles to decide what your specific succulents need. Bear in mind that many cacti actually need a period of cold dormancy if you want them to flower.

Below Only a few succulents will survive a frost. If you want one to live outside, check the range of temperatures it will tolerate before you plant.

EXCEPTIONS TO THE RULE

Epiphytic cacti, natives of tropical forests, don't follow the growth/dormancy pattern of most other desert-living succulents. Instead, they grow in spring, become dormant over the summer and go into active growth again in the autumn. They also tend to prefer semi-shade conditions to full sun. They flower – often flamboyantly – at the end of winter and into the start of spring, when not much else is in bloom. The *Epiphyllum*, *Schlumbergera* and *Rhipsalis* groups – which include such popular plants as the fishbone cactus, *Epiphyllum anguliger* (see pp.90–91); the Mistletoe cactus, *Rhipsalis baccifera* (see pp.100–101); and the Christmas cactus, *Schlumbergera* × *buckleyi* (see p.103) – all belong in this category.

Christmas cactus
Schlumbergera × *buckleyi*

KEEPING PLANTS HEALTHY AND TIDY

A weekly check-up and maintenance session will keep your succulents looking good and bring out their subtle textures and colours. Many will benefit from an occasional trim or a light prune, too, to get rid of any damaged stems or foliage and give them a better shape.

CLEANING UP

All houseplants benefit from a weekly check-up and clean. With a smooth-surfaced succulent, like a crassula or an echeveria, you can wipe down the stems and leaves with a soft, dry cloth. With a spiky or hairy plant, a mammillaria cactus, for example, you'll need to bring out your small paintbrushes; an angled one will help dislodge dust from prickly corners,

and a round artist's brush will sweep away the debris. A close look will also ensure that you spot any lurking pests (see p.53) before they multiply. Every so often, tip out the gravel or pebbles that are top-dressing your pots and give it a wash. Dry it carefully before redistributing back at the top of the pot. Keeping both the plants and their containers really clean and dust- and dirt-free ensures they never get that neglected aura which can make your whole interior look tired.

TRIMMING AND PRUNING

Clear away fallen leaves from your succulents as soon as you notice them; in many plants, the lower foliage will fall off as the plant grows bigger and the stem hardens. Gently pull off leaves that are withered or discoloured when you come across them, too.

Sometimes you'll want to carry out slightly more significant surgery. Perhaps there's a side branch on your plant that doesn't seem to be thriving although the plant seems healthy overall, or the shape of the plant has changed as a lot of side stems have emerged and it's all starting

to look a bit bushy and messy. Use sharp scissors or pruning shears for trimming or pruning, so that you won't leave ragged edges, and disinfect the blades by wiping them with surgical spirit (rubbing alcohol) before cutting. If you're pruning for cosmetic reasons, stand back from the plant and look at it carefully before cutting, to ensure you're clear about the bits you want to remove, otherwise it may end up with a too-dramatic haircut as you over-correct your first mistake.

Above and below Be cautious when trimming for shape – it's easy to overdo it. Damaged growth, though, should be removed as soon as you spot it, using sharp pruning shears or scissors. Left on too long, it can spread rot across the plant.

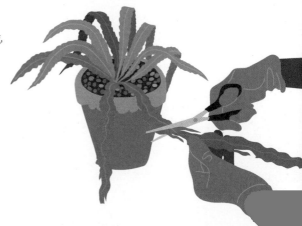

WATERING AND FEEDING

Because cacti and succulents have evolved to store water in their stems and leaves, they don't need the soil around their roots to be constantly damp. This means that they can – and usually should – be left to dry out thoroughly between waterings. But it doesn't mean that they can do without water completely.

KILLING WITH KINDNESS

The idea that succulents can be left alone for long periods isn't necessarily wrong. Most originate from desert conditions and are used to occasional droughts, and those kept as houseplants are still probably more often killed by overwatering than by neglect. You need to know when to water, and how (it's not as obvious as you might think), and when to leave well alone.

USING RAINWATER

It's best to use room-temperature rainwater for watering. Some species can be sensitive to the chemicals in water from the tap. If you don't have access to an outdoor water butt, leave a bowl outside to collect water you can use, and leave it to warm to room temperature before you use it, to avoid giving your plants a chilly shock. If you don't have any way to collect rainwater, run tap water and let it stand for a couple of days before using it to water your plants.

DIFFERENT NEEDS

There are two main considerations when it comes to how often you should water: which group a succulent belongs to, and whether or not it's dormant. While no succulent needs constant watering, some are thirstier than others. And all of them need more regular watering when they're in active growth than during dormancy.

The forest-dwelling epiphytic cacti are, as always, the exceptions in the group. They need more regular watering than desert succulents, and can be watered, sparingly, even when the soil in their pots is still slightly moist; as a general rule, water them once a week, draining well in between. The majority of succulents, though, the desert-dwellers, should only be watered when their soil has dried out thoroughly – when you push the top two joints of your finger into the soil of a pot, it should feel dry to the touch. Limp, yellowing leaves and soft spots on the stems are signs that you could be watering your plants too much.

Succulents need watering only very rarely, if at all, while they're dormant (see pp.38–9). Most enter dormancy in later autumn, and stay dormant through winter, but there are exceptions (epiphytic cacti are usually dormant in the summer), so check the specific information for a species if you're not sure.

Above Overwatering is far more of a threat to succulents than the reverse. If a succulent's roots are sitting in water for any length of time, it can collapse very suddenly, without hope of revival.

Can dry ever be too dry? Yes – if you notice that the stems or leaves of your succulents are starting to wrinkle or wither, they need watering. As always, let them drain thoroughly afterward and leave them to dry out again.

THE BEST WAY TO WATER

If you've only ever happily sloshed water over annuals out in a border or in pots, a 'best method' may come as a surprise. There are a couple of reasons why you need to be more careful with succulents. First, if water is splashed over the leaves it can mark them, or, if they're in direct sun,

leave scorch marks, and spoil the subtle colour and texture which are a large part of many succulents' charm. Second, the pots mustn't be left standing in water, so if your plants sit in saucers or outer 'sleeve' containers, these should be emptied and dried after you've watered. A top dressing of gravel or pebbles in pots should avoid the stems or leaves being left in contact with the soil while it's still damp. If you're watering hanging baskets, it's often easier to take them down and let them drain over a tray on the floor rather than trying to catch drips that might fall on your carpets or furniture.

Use a small indoor watering can with a long, narrow spout and aim the water directly into the soil, away from contact with the plant; stop watering when drips start to come out of the drainage holes at the bottom. The open nature of the potting medium you've used will mean that water flows through the container quite fast.

Don't suddenly stop watering as plants enter dormancy; instead, tail it off as the dormant season approaches, watering less often, and with less water.

Above Water according to the size of the pot and plant: with your littlest succulents, it may be easier to give them a drink with a large syringe than with a small watering can.

FEEDING SUCCULENTS

The commercial potting soil marketed specifically for cacti and succulents usually also contains a dose of appropriate fertilizer, but the home mix you make doesn't. Although succulents don't need much feeding – and, rather like too much water, too much fertilizer can do them more harm than good – a once-a-month feed during their growing season should help to keep your plants strong and healthy. Just as with potting soils, there are commercial feeds sold specially for succulents, and these are usually slightly lower in nitrogen than ordinary houseplant fertilizers; the latter tend to have evenly balanced quantities of nitrogen, potassium and phosphorus. You can use one of the specialist fertilizers or pick a tomato feed – which will be high in potassium – or a general all-round feed for houseplants. If you opt for one of the latter, make a weaker solution: check the recommended dose and double the dilution suggested.

REPOTTING

While many container plants need to be moved into a larger container annually, succulents are generally slow growers and don't need a lot of extra space around their roots, so you may find that they only need repotting every two or three years.

HOW YOU KNOW REPOTTING IS DUE

If you're not sure whether or not your succulent needs repotting, start by looking at the drainage holes in the base of the container – if the roots are growing through them, it's probably time to repot.

Carefully shake the container to loosen the soil and slide the plant out, using your cactus gloves or a cactus collar (see p.17) to handle it if it's spiky. Push any gravel or pebbles you've used as top dressing to one side – you can re-use them in the new pot. If the soil ball doesn't come out easily, gently run a blunt-bladed knife down the inside and around the edges of the container. Once the plant is out, look at the roots. If they're very tightly packed and are starting to grow in circles around one another, the plant is root bound and it's definitely time to move it on.

WATER BEFORE REPOTTING

It's easier to settle your plant into new potting soil if it's been watered fairly recently, so if you're going to move a succulent to a new container, water it a few days before you repot it, leaving it to drain thoroughly afterward as usual.

MOVING ON

The new container should be one, or at most two, sizes bigger than the one the plant is in – so if the pot it's in is 20cm (8in) diameter, say, pick a 22.5cm (9in) diameter pot, or at most a 25cm (10in) diameter one to move it into. Use either a commercial cactus mix or your own mixture and a small – indoor – trowel or a metal kitchen spoon to move it into the container. Spoon enough fresh potting soil into the base of the new pot for the plant, sitting on it, to come up to within an inch of the top of the pot, then centre the plant in the space and add potting soil around the sides, pushing it down gently, until the container is full (don't push down hard, or you'll compact the soil which will mean that it won't drain as effectively). Finish by adding a top dressing of grit, gravel or small stones around the plant.

Above If, when you take the plant out of its pot, the roots are compacted, like the one shown above, gently squeeze the root ball to loosen them slightly so that they don't carry on growing in a choking circle inside the new pot.

ENCOURAGING FLOWERS

Full disclosure first: not every succulent that is kept as a houseplant will flower. Many will, but some need conditions that it's just not possible for you to supply at home. So if your heart is set on a flowering succulent, read the plant profile carefully in order to avoid buyer's remorse.

WILL THEY, WON'T THEY?

Agaves, for example, are highly unlikely to flower when kept indoors (though you might think that their impressively sculptural looks make up for that). Likewise, *Cephalocereus senilis*, the old man cactus, which has pretty night-scented flowers when it's growing in the wild, is very unlikely to flower at home.

If its profile confirms that in theory the plant will flower indoors, here's how to encourage it to perform in practice. First, make sure it's in good health, and that it's old enough. Many succulents won't flower until they're fully mature, and as most tend to be slow-growing and long-lived in any case, if your plant is young and small, you may have a few years to wait. If it's old enough, do your best to give it an annual break in the form of a dormant period; in their natural habitat, succulents flower in the season after dormancy. Finally, there's a short cut – if you want to be certain, it's possible to buy succulents that are already in flower.

Left Maturity is often an important factor in whether or not a succulent will flower. If you start with a small, young plant, you may need to wait a year or two for it to bloom.

FOUR EASY BLOOMERS

While no succulent comes with an absolute guarantee, here are some that can usually be depended on to flower.

1 Rat's tail cactus (*Disocactus flagelliformis*) A spring-flowering trailing cactus, with large deep-red or pink flowers. Good for a hanging basket.

2 *Echeveria* species Many of this rosette-forming group flower readily, although the flowers themselves vary widely from small and delicate to large and gaudy, depending on the species.

3 *Mammillaria* species Most of these round, prickly cacti will flower regularly; the flowers, which come in shades of red, pink, white or cream, often bloom in a crown-like ring around the top of the plant.

4 Christmas cactus (*Schlumbergera × buckleyi*) A willing and prolific bloomer with flamboyant flowers in shades of purple, red or pink, carried in early to mid-winter after a summer dormancy. Good for a hanging basket.

TROUBLESHOOTING

When succulents have problems, these can be broadly divided into three categories. A plant may be in a less-than-ideal situation – it's too hot or too cool, or has too much light, or not enough, or has been over- or under-watered. It may be suffering from a condition or disease, such as rot or a fungal problem. Or, finally, it may be under attack from a pest. One may affect another; for example, an overwatered plant may not only rot but also fall prey to fungus. First you need to spot the problem, then diagnose it, and finally decide how to treat it: here's how.

MAKING A DIAGNOSIS

If you're already giving your plants a sprucing-up session once a week, you should spot problems early. Include hanging baskets in your clean-and-check routine, either taking them down to look at them, or climbing up to their level.

PROBLEMS WITH A PLANT'S SITUATION

Sometimes a plant isn't suited to its living quarters, and since plants can't get up and walk away, it's your job to spot the problem. The three basics to check on are whether the plant is getting the right amount of water and light, and whether it is warm enough or – more rarely – too warm.

	What you see	What you should do
OVER/UNDER WATERING	Overwatering, and leaving a plant's potting soil too damp, can cause rot. Early signs are soft, yellowing leaves and soft spots on the stems. Underwatering can cause leaves to shrivel and wither. An underwatered plant may also drop flower buds before they open, and halt growing completely.	Remove plants from their pots. If a plant is too wet, check the roots aren't rotting and leave it to dry out away from its pot. Cut any root rot away. When the plant has dried out, repot it into new potting soil. If a plant is too dry, replace it in its pot and sit it in a water-filled saucer to let it rehydrate thoroughly. When the soil at the top of the pot is damp, remove the saucer.
NOT ENOUGH LIGHT/ TOO MUCH LIGHT	A plant in too low a light will become pale and spindly, and grow one-sided, toward what light is available. A plant in too strong a light may develop pale or brown withered patches, a sign of so-called 'leaf scorch' – plant sunburn.	Place a plant suffering from too little light in the sunniest spot you can find; shade a plant in too-strong light slightly with a thin curtain if it's in a window, or move it slightly further into the room, where the light isn't so strong.
TOO HOT/ TOO COLD	A too-hot plant will dry out very quickly after watering, and may look withered or shrivelled. A plant that's kept in a draught, especially by a window where temperatures may drop suddenly at night, may develop brown spots on its leaves or stems.	Treat an overheated plant like one that's getting too much light: move it further from its light source. Make sure it's nowhere near a radiator. Move a plant that's too cold away from any draughts or, if it's on a windowsill, away from condensation on the window, which, being both cold and wet, is particularly damaging.

Opposite A weekly check will ensure that you spot any key changes in your plants. Some species shed their lower leaves naturally as they grow; with others, a change in colour or a softening of the foliage can warn of a problem. The brown spots on the leaves of this *Aloe vera* are a sign of overwatering.

TROUBLESHOOTING DISEASES

Diseases in succulents usually come about from a combination of factors. Many can be treated, but you may then have to change a watering routine or the plant's location to make sure the issue doesn't arise again.

	What you see	What you should do
ROOT ROT	The succulent wilts before collapsing.	If you catch it at the wilting stage, the treatment is to remove it from its pot, trim off any evidently soft, rotting roots, and leave to dry out, as with overwatering, before repotting into fresh potting soil.
BASAL STEM ROT	Soft brown, damp-looking areas at the root of the plant; wilting stems and leaves.	It's not good news, unfortunately – once basal stem rot is bad enough to be visible, the plant will die. The rot can be the result of a number of problems: the plant may have had inadequate drainage or been overwatered, or its conditions may be too humid. Sometimes you can cut off a top leaf or stem and use them to propagate a new plant, but the parent plant should be thrown away.
CORKY SCAB	Brown raised patches with a woody, 'corky' texture on a succulent's leaves.	Corky scab arises when a plant is kept in over-humid conditions and doesn't have enough air circulating around it. Put it in a bright, well-ventilated spot and cut down on watering.
FUNGAL LEAF SPOT	Brown or black spots on a plant's stem and leaves.	Leaf spot is caused by a fungus, usually as a result of too much humidity, poor air circulation or careless, splashy watering. Take off affected leaves or stems if possible, and re-site the plant in a drier, airier spot.
GREY MOULD	Furry grey patches, often at the base of a plant's leaves.	Grey mould is serious – usually the result of too much damp or humidity – but if you've caught it early, the plant may survive if you take off all the affected leaves or stems as quickly as possible, and quarantine it in a bright spot to dry out thoroughly.

TROUBLESHOOTING PESTS

There aren't all that many pests that will afflict a plant kept indoors. The four that you're most likely to encounter are mealybugs, scale insects, red spider mites and thrips. They all suck the sap of your succulents and cause varying degrees of damage.

	What you see	What they are	What you should do
MEALYBUGS	Fluffy, woolly-looking patches on the surfaces of plants.	These are secretions from mealybugs. Left on a plant, they cause it to become weak and to grow in a distorted shape. They also excrete sticky honeydew, which is a problem in its own right as it can cause deposits of black sooty mould.	You can buy a targeted pesticide spray to get rid of a mealybug infestation, but if the problem isn't extensive, dip a cotton bud (cotton swab) in surgical spirit (rubbing alcohol), available from pharmacies, and meticulously go over the plant, wiping the secretions and any mould away. Check other plants nearby and treat them too if necessary.
SCALE INSECTS	Tiny, flat oval-shaped 'scales', which can range from brown to pale green, usually collected around the ribs or joints of a plant where they're harder to spot.	Scale insects have a protective shell-like cover, damaging plants by sucking the sap and, like mealybugs, excreting honeydew, which can cause sooty mould.	As with the treatment for mealybugs, you can go over the afflicted plant carefully with a cotton bud (cotton swab) and surgical spirit (rubbing alcohol). If the infestation is heavy, you can buy a targeted pesticide spray.
RED SPIDER MITES	Pale brown or off-white blotches on the new growth of a plant, which quickly spreads over a wider area, and is followed by misshapen new stems and leaves.	Red spider mites are very tiny – and are more often pale green than red – but they can cause serious, disproportionate damage if they're not caught fast. You can hardly see them, but they do create very fine webs, like spiderwebs, which are more easily visible.	Spray with a targeted pesticide and if just one part of a plant is affected and it's possible to trim it off, do so. Keep a recovering plant in an airy place: spider mites like hot, still conditions so the better ventilated a plant is, the better. Quarantine an affected plant in a different room so others aren't infected.
THRIPS	Spotty brown discolouration or pale, withered patches on leaves and stems.	Tiny flies and their young (you may see them flying if you pick up the plant and gently shake it).	Spray with a targeted pesticide. You can also buy traps for thrips, similar to those available for clothes moths, but although these will stop them from multiplying, they won't deal with their young.

CHAPTER THREE

Showing Off Your Plants

You've already fallen for the charms of succulents and learned the basics of where to buy them and how to look after them; the next part, for many enthusiasts, is the most enjoyable – looking at the various different ways in which you can show them off. There are plants in this group to fit all interiors, whether you're after a sculptural statement that will turn a dull corner into a visual high point, or a collection of smaller plants with an engaging variety of textures, forms and colours, ready to be curated in various different ways to fit your style and your living space.

There's always a way to give plants a fresh look, and trying out different containers and groupings can become addictive. If you love a project, this chapter offers plenty of ideas for you to try, too, from a succulent dish landscape and a neat terrarium – improvised from a preserving (canning) jar – to a trio of hanging baskets and some striking table centrepieces.

WINDOWSILL ARRANGEMENTS

A sunny windowsill is an excellent location for most of the desert-dwelling species – care-wise, all you need to keep an eye on is that they don't get too hot at the height of summer or take a chill if they're shut behind curtains on a cold winter's night. And even the simplest line-up of pots of succulents or cacti has the potential to look casually stylish.

SET DRESSING

If you want to change the heights of plants, raise pots up on stacks of hardback books (use some of the nicely bound but otherwise uninteresting books that are available for pence at thrift shops, rather than risking water or soil stains on your own treasured library). Mix in plants with stones and pebbles, feathers and twigs; this sort of random, grown-up-nature-table approach can have a real tactile charm. Alternatively, go for an arrangement of extreme precision, using matching containers to make even a disparate group of plants look connected.

Above Use a tray with a lip to contain a windowsill arrangement consisting of multiple small pots – it's a visual unifier and makes it easy to move them around.

INDOOR WINDOW BOXES

Window boxes and planters need not be confined to the garden; indoors, they're a good way of unifying what might otherwise seem to be a rather random selection of plants, raising it to the status of a curated, considered collection. You can make your own if you enjoy a bit of simple woodwork and want it made to measure, or shop around to find one that suits. If you don't want to spend too much, plastic window boxes are very easy to disguise with paint, and you can get plastic paint in a lot of non-tacky finishes – there's even a spray-on chalkboard option.

Unless your plants are quite large, it's best to use the window box as an outer container rather than to plant them directly into it, as there's likely to be too much room for the roots of smaller succulents. If necessary, use blocks or props inside the box to raise individual pots so they line up, and encourage branches to trail if that's their habit, to loosen up the overall effect.

GLASS SHELVES

Glass shelves across a window can be used to screen off an unappealing view without compromising the amount of light that comes into a room, and objects placed on them seem to float. Fitting them isn't difficult, although it's also not always a simple process – you'll need to fit brackets into the window rebate. In the right space, though, they're worth considering: they can make a wonderful display space for your succulents.

Below When grouping small succulents, try to create an appealing patchwork within the container.

PROJECT: MAKING A SUCCULENT DISH LANDSCAPE

There's something very appealing about the idea of a miniature landscape on your table. A succulent garden planted into a large, shallow dish is a popular classic, and you can add props according to taste – you might aim for something fun and kitsch, or subtle and elegant, or even a little surreal.

MINIATURE WORLDS

Your dish can be plain earthenware or something a bit fancier, but it must have drainage holes. For the best landscape effect, don't plant it too densely; group the plants, but leave some top-dressed 'ground' clear. Choose plants either from the same group or from different groups that have similar needs – for example, you could use just echeverias, or mix them up with some sedums or sempervivums. Your succulent landscape should be hardy enough to live outdoors during the warmer months if you'd like, although you may want to bring it indoors when the temperatures drop.

YOU WILL NEED

- A broad, shallow dish, about 30cm (12in) in diameter and 7.5cm (3in) tall

- A bag of commercial succulent potting soil, or your own mix (see pp.26–7)

- Large metal spoon

- Between five and seven small succulents, averaging around 7.5cm (3in) diameter – one or two smaller or larger plants will add to the uneven 'landscape' effect

- A few small clumps of moss (optional)

- White gravel, to top-dress the pot after planting

- A few small models or other props

1 Add a layer of potting soil at the base of your dish using the spoon, then place your succulents and move them around until you're happy with the arrangement – check it from the side, as well as from above, to make sure the whole effect is pleasing. When you are happy, gently fill in the gaps with soil.

2 Add the gravel as a top dressing, smoothing it neatly around the plant stems, so that it makes an even, level layer.

3 Place small clumps of moss, if using, around the landscape to resemble smaller clumps of plants.

4 Time to place the props. A landscape dish for a child might include small dinosaurs placed on the open areas of the gravel, or models of a cowboy and their horse making their way across the 'desert'. Alternatively, one or two largeish shells, arranged against a piece of bleached white driftwood will work with the colours and textures of the succulents for a more sophisticated effect.

5 Place the dish on a sunny windowsill or tabletop. You could swap the props around or even exchange one or two of the plants every so often, to keep the look fresh.

PLANT GROUPINGS TO TRY

For a mix of rosette forms with different colours and textures:

- Green pinwheel (*Aeonium decorum*)
- Moulded wax 'Taurus' (*Echeveria agavoides* 'Taurus')
- Cobweb houseleek (*Sempervivum arachnoideum*)

For a dish of 'specimen' cacti. (Like all desert dwellers, they will need to be kept very dry):

- Emory's barrel cactus (*Ferocactus emoryi*)
- Devil's tongue cactus (*Ferocactus latispinus*)
- Golden ball cactus (*Parodia leninghausii*)

For a larger dish, these plants grow comparatively fast and can get quite big:

- Donkey's tail (*Sedum morganianum*)
- Moulded wax 'Taurus' (*Echeveria agavoides* 'Taurus')
- Jade plant (*Crassula ovata*)

USING PLANT STANDS

Plant stands can be a helpful solution if you have limited floor space or an awkward corner to fill, and a lot of plants to display. They come in plenty of shapes and sizes, from purpose-designed to improvised, and from the classic triangular three-shelf wrought-iron version, more often seen full of geraniums than succulents, to modern designs made of every imaginable material, from wood to slate.

FROM FANCY TO SIMPLE

Purpose-made plant stands can be hunted out in all kinds of places. Check out your local auction room; garden and outdoor ephemera sales often have elaborate jardinières, old terracotta chimney pots and other oddball pieces that can make wonderful one-of-a-kind plant stands. If you have simpler tastes, most garden centres and DIY stores sell a variety of more basic (and cheaper) options. You can improvise with everyday household items such as step-stools or mini three- or four-step stepladders, too; folded down or opened out, these make effective and economical multilevel stands.

Left Keep an eye out for unexpected items that can be repurposed into plant stands.

IMPROVISED STAND IDEAS

There's a wide range of options you can use for display, found everywhere from the thrift store to your local woodyard. Here are just three ideas, very different from one another, but all equally effective.

Cut log sections A local tree surgeon or woodyard will often be able to sell you lengths of log. Ask for the bark to be left on if you want the maximum rustic effect, and buy three, cut to different lengths, to make impromptu plant stands (they're particularly effective for larger plants).

Hostess trolley Since they've become popular recycled as drinks carts, a wheeled 1970s hostess trolley may no longer be the super-cheap option it once was, but it makes a great two-or-three level plant stand for small- to medium-sized plants. It's easily moved from place to place, and if you're well organized you may even be able to combine the two functions stylishly – drinks served from one end, succulents displayed at the other.

Stool 'nests' Usually sold for inexpensive emergency seating, these stools tend to come in trios, each stacking into the next size up, so at three slightly different heights. They're simple, plain designs, often made from plywood, and a nest makes an excellent trio of neat, streamlined plant stands.

PROJECT: MAKING A TERRARIUM IN A JAR

This simple terrarium, planted in a preserving (canning) jar, is easy to put together and makes a great gift. Don't leave the lid on for any length of time; open terrariums are a good way to show off succulents, but the closed type isn't suitable, because the condensation may cause the plants to rot.

A 2-litre (64oz) preserving jar is a good size to start with: it's large enough to ensure that it is not too fiddly to plant up, but small enough to be easily moved around. You could centre the planting on a small aloe (perhaps *Aloe aristata* or *A. humilis*) for a spiky shape, or a mammillaria (*Mammillaria longiflora*, the pincushion cactus, would look good) if you want a round silhouette. Use a couple of slightly smaller plants to accompany the star plant – most sedum species would work well here.

YOU WILL NEED

- A 2-litre (64oz) preserving (canning) jar
- Plants (see opposite page)
- Gravel or small pebbles
- A bag of commercial succulent potting soil, or your own mix (see pp.26–7)
- Pair of small kitchen tongs
- Large metal spoon
- Wooden spoon

1 Wash, rinse and thoroughly dry the jar you're using for your terrarium.

2 Use the metal spoon to add a layer of gravel or pebbles in the base, about 5cm (2in) deep, and shake the jar to level it.

3 Spoon in a layer of potting soil, about 7.5cm (3in) deep, using the metal spoon, and level it off with the back of the spoon.

4 Using the wooden spoon gently, so as not to compact the soil too much, make three hollows – one in the middle, for your main plant, the other two for its smaller companions. Next, use the tongs to lower first the main plant, then the other two, into the hollows. Finally, adjust the soil around the plants and firm them in lightly, using the wooden spoon.

5 To transport, or give as a gift, screw the top of the jar on. Once the jar is in place, the lid should be removed to allow air to circulate. Water only occasionally; you may find it easier to use a baster than a watering can, so the water can be directed away from the plants.

RECYCLING BROKEN POTS

If you've amassed a collection of broken or cracked terracotta pots – and most container gardeners have a stash of them – one effective and appealing way you can put them to work is to use them to make a broken-pot garden for succulents.

NEW POTS FOR OLD

A broken-pot garden is just as it sounds – pieces of earthenware pots are fitted into one another in order to make a stepped planting container, with succulents planted in at several levels. You need plenty of different pot bits to start with, including a large base piece (most of a pot, with only one side broken away) to anchor the finished composition and keep it stable. The construction process is a little like building a rock garden, but with pots – you add a layer of potting soil into the base of the largest pot, balance another one or two pieces in it, leaving a little planting space at the side, then carry on filling hollows with soil, adding a plant where you can. When it's done well, you'll achieve an end effect that looks like an effortless cornucopia – a composition that's generously spilling out plants on all sides. It's slightly trickier to do than it looks, though, so check through the tips before you start.

Below When you're constructing a broken-pot garden, mix some upright plants with others that will droop or trail over the edges.

MAKING YOUR RECYCLED POT CONTAINER WORK

Collect a selection of different sizes of broken pots before you start (if you haven't had enough pot disasters yourself, gardening friends and family should be able to help). The large base piece is an essential ingredient; once that's in place, pieces of smaller pots, including some other base pieces, can be fitted in.

Jade necklace/string of buttons
(*Crassula marnieriana*)

When it comes to choosing plants, most suitably sized aeoniums, sedums and crassulas will work well. The finished effect will be enhanced if you can add one or two trailing plants which will hang down the sides. There are lots of options, but check out *Crassula marnieriana* or *Sedum makinoi* 'Tornado', both of which have chunky little spreading branches with a slightly trailing habit.

Japanese stonecrop
(*Sedum makinoi*)

Check out the stability of your arrangement, rocking the pots slightly as you go, and packing in soil and smaller shards to balance it overall.

USING STATEMENT PLANTS

Some spots at home don't lend themselves to grouped arrangements. Maybe there isn't much floor space – alongside a door, with furniture nearby, for example – or maybe it just seems to call for a single, eye-catching plant. As anyone who has visited the glasshouses of a great botanical garden can tell you, this is where the sculptural look of succulents comes into its own.

GOING LARGER

If you're used to the small-scale appeal of a succulent dish or a terrarium, buying something much larger – and more expensive – will feel like a substantial investment. If you know that you're looking for a bigger, more mature plant it may be the right moment to pay a visit to a specialist nursery, where you'll generally find more to choose from, along with information on tap about the right plant for your circumstances and how to keep it well and happy when you get it home. Of course, there's nothing to stop you nurturing a smaller plant (of one of the larger species) to an impressive maturity, but because succulents are slow growing, you'll need to prepare yourself for quite a long wait.

LARGER PLANTS

Check out where a statement plant will go, and measure how much space you've got before going shopping. Think of how a plant might look on its own small stand in the place you have in mind for it; if it's not tall enough, you may need to raise it to give it enough light and to 'place' it in your room.

2

Left Golden barrel cactus (*Echinocactus grusonii*)

THREE GOOD STATEMENT PLANTS

1 Silver torch cactus (*Cleistocactus strausii*) The silver torch cactus can reach 50cm (20in) or more, even when kept as an indoor plant. It has fine, silvery spikes that reflect the light, and the grouped columns look like everyone's idea of a Western-movie cactus.

2 Golden barrel cactus (*Echinocactus grusonii*) A large, round globe of a cactus covered in spines that can grow up to 60cm × 60cm (24in × 24in), a well-grown golden barrel cactus looks great as a single statement piece displayed on a coffee table.

3 Bunny ears cactus (*Opuntia microdasys*) The flat oval paddles that branch off one another – the 'bunny ears' – are highly characteristic of most *Opuntia* species. This one is striking to look at and grows to a manageable 60cm (24in); it looks good on a standalone plant stand. Although it's spineless, its soft bristles can irritate the skin, so always handle with gloves.

Top Silver torch cactus (*Cleistocactus strausii*)
Bottom Bunny ears cactus (*Opuntia microdasys*)

PROJECT:
A TRIO OF HANGING BASKETS

For this project, we're using a 'three-in-one' hanging basket, all three baskets lushly planted up with epiphytic cacti – also known as tropical, or orchid cacti. These are the succulents that prefer semi-shade to full sun and also like a higher degree of humidity than desert-living species, so the baskets could work well in a bathroom, as well as in other spaces which have less direct light.

FOLIAGE AND FLOWERS

Shop around for favourites to fill the baskets or consider some (or all!) of the options listed below. Choose smaller examples of the plants you pick (some epiphyte species grow quite big), and use the smallest in the top basket, and the biggest in the lowest, larger one.

The following five all offer the good looks needed, and given the right conditions, will also flower spectacularly:

Rat's tail cactus (*Disocactus flagelliformis*) (p.88)

Fishbone cactus (*Epiphyllum anguliger*) (pp.90–91)

Hurricane cactus (*Lepismium cruciforme*) – flattened wavy stems that have white, hair-like tufts along their length (pictured above left)

Easter cactus (*Hatiora gaertneri*) – broad stems that have strongly defined segments

Mistletoe cactus (*Rhipsalis baccifera*) (pp.100–101) (pictured below left)

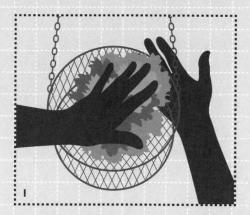

1

YOU WILL NEED

• A trio of wire baskets, each
  hanging below the other, with
  the smallest at the top and the
  largest below

• Commercial succulent potting soil,
  or your own mix (see pp.26–7)

• Moss for lining the baskets (you
  can collect this yourself, or buy
  it, see p.24)

• Large metal kitchen spoon

• A choice of epiphytic plants –
  the five listed opposite will work
  well; if you opt for alternatives,
  make sure they belong to the
  tropical cactus group

1 Hang the baskets from a secure,
lowish point – hook them to the back
of a chair or a solid shelf. Soak a handful
of moss in water for a minute or two,
then squeeze the water out and press the
moss around the inside of the top basket.
Repeat, a handful at a time, until the
basket is fully lined.

2 Repeat step 1 to line the lower two
baskets, then leave the moss liners to
dry out for a few hours.

3 Fill all three baskets with a potting soil
mixture suitable for your chosen plants
(see pp.26–27).

4 Arrange your plants in the baskets,
using a metal spoon to dig out a hollow
for each of them. You can stay simple, with
just one plant per basket, or mix them up,
with two or three small plants in each.

5 Water the baskets, draining them over
a tray, before hanging them in the spot
you've chosen.

CENTREPIECES

From time to time, you may want to use some of your plants centre-stage to make an impact – putting together a centrepiece for a special meal, say, or to decorate for a celebration or a birthday. If you don't want to go to the trouble of repotting or making major rearrangements to plants that are happy as they are, it's simple enough to dress things up temporarily.

USING CANDLES

The combination of succulents and candlelight works really well on a festive dining table or side-table arrangement. The flickering light brings out the subtleties of the plants' colours and textures, but you'll still want to avoid wax drips or scorch marks on the leaves and stems. Bring candles and plants together visually by using dishes of sand (you can sink small container plants into it, then add the candle or candles in a separate pot or container); alternatively, group the plants around a glass hurricane lantern with the candle inside.

If you have mostly smaller plants, consider lining them up along the middle of the table and alternating them with nightlights, using matching containers for both succulents and candles. Small mirrored nightlight-holders, for example, holding little round cacti, such as mammillaria species, make a striking effect without much outlay. Used horizontal rather than hung, a flat wreath frame in wicker or woven bamboo also makes a good base for small potted succulents; in winter, you can mix up the containers alongside other greenery such as holly and mistletoe for a seasonal effect.

SHOWCASING CONTAINERS

Swapping the containers your plants are in can make a big difference to the atmosphere they bring. Instead of pots, try using vases — the kind of containers you might use for fresh cut flowers — as 'sleeves' for your plants. You may find that the contrast is surprisingly successful. Alternatively, group similar containers around or onto a shared base: a tray, a long piece of driftwood (often sold in florists' stores), or a piece of slate can all work well.

Below and opposite Not only do succulents make attractive table settings, you can also use them to hold place cards or even dress them up as party favours.

CHAPTER FOUR

Plant Profiles

This chapter looks at a number of succulent and cacti species in detail, to help you when you're choosing plants. Every species included has earned a potential space in your home, out on your balcony or in a sheltered corner of your garden, and all of them are fully described and illustrated, with an overview of the care they will need to thrive.

Two practical points to remember. First, the size given in each plant's profile is the maximum height and spread you would usually expect it to reach when it's growing as a houseplant – many species would grow much bigger in their native habitat. As previously mentioned, most succulents are slow to grow and, even when you're caring for it devotedly, it can still take a long time for a young, small plant to reach its mature size. If you would like a larger plant and want to avoid a long wait, it may make sense for you to buy a larger one to start with.

Second is a safety consideration, which bears repeating: many succulents are toxic if they're eaten, so please be careful – they should be kept well out of reach of small children and pets. And of course many of them are spiky, too; make sure that plants with sharp spines are placed where they can't hurt anyone.

HOW TO CHOOSE WHAT YOU'LL GROW

When you start keeping succulents, the choice available is always enticing. There is such a huge range, so many different looks, sizes, colours... So check out all the qualities you like, but remember to be realistic about your circumstances, too. Since there are succulents and cacti for almost every situation, it's best to look for those that are a good match.

CHECK BEFORE YOU BUY

If you're preparing for a browse through the profiles section, followed by a shopping trip, answer the following questions first; they'll clarify what you should be looking for.

How much space do you have?

If you're limited for space, look at how much you can spare for plants. Do you have a windowsill? Or a side-table? If you have bookshelves, could you make space on them to show off one or two plants, as you would photos or collectibles? If you honestly don't have space for any big contenders, concentrate on the smaller options, many of which have a miniature charm of their own (check out the mammillarias on pp.98–9, for example).

How much light do you have?

If your living space is shady, and you don't have too much direct light, don't look at the extreme desert-dwellers; you don't have the circumstances for them to thrive. Instead, look at tropical cacti, such as Christmas cactus (*Schlumbergera*) or *Rhipsalis* species or, if trailing plants are less to your taste, aeoniums, despite their sun-loving reputation, will often manage quite well in indirect light, or even partial shade.

How warm is it?

When you're at home, you probably make sure that it's warm enough to be comfortable. However, if you're out at work, and the heating isn't on, it may get considerably colder on a winter's day.

And if you have heat-loving plants on a windowsill and they get shut behind curtains overnight, they may get cold and damp. It's worth checking temperatures at all times of day with a thermometer if you're not sure – don't forget, your plants can't get up and move somewhere warmer if they're placed in a draught. Check out echeverias, sedums and sempervivums for some species that will cope with chillier (and sometimes even damper) surroundings than sun-hungry cacti, for example.

Above Cacti species that originate from the desert rather than the forest need at least four hours of bright, direct light daily, so a sunny windowsill is often an ideal spot for them.

GROWING OUTDOORS

If most of your growing space is indoors, it can be easy to forget that many succulents will manage to live outside quite happily at least for the warmer months of the year. Some will even cope year-round – remember that many green roofs (see pp.78–79) are planted up with succulents, and most of those will tough it through a chilly winter and still look good in spring.

WET AND COLD

Most succulents that are resilient enough to live outdoors are at more threat from wet than cold. In summer, many container plants will happily enjoy outdoor life provided that their drainage is good enough to make sure their roots don't sit in water after rain. Succulent pots of sedums, sempervivums and aeoniums can often be left outside year-round without coming to any harm, provided that they're planted in light, free-draining potting soil in the first place and are raised so that any additional water drains off them. Unless they're in a very sheltered spot, though, they may not always survive a hard frost.

Above. Those succulents that can overwinter outdoors may need extra help to drain off heavy rainfall – avoid plant saucers and raise the pots on pot feet instead.

TOUGH CUSTOMERS

If you specifically want to grow cacti outdoors, be aware that it's risky: generally, they're even less likely to bear damp than most other succulents. If you're detemined to live dangerously, the *Opuntia* species are the most likely cacti to cope with the outdoor life if you can give them shelter, light and excellent drainage. There are, however, a number of larger succulents in other groups that, planted in the right spot, can be happy living outside, in a bed rather than a container, for the long term. The aloes and agaves listed below need to be planted with some care – aim for a fairly sheltered spot and plant them into very gritty potting soil, ideally overlaid with a layer of gravel. Treated well, they make handsome, sizeable additions that are worth taking a little care over.

ALOES

As mature plants, several aloes are hardy enough to live outside. Two that are outstanding in terms of looks are lace aloe (*Aloe aristata*) and the many-leaved aloe (*A. polyphylla*). Both form the beautiful Fibonacci-spiralled rosettes that are characteristic of the family – *A. aristata* has spiny paler edges to its leaves and, in spring, will throw up a tall spike that carries red, tubular flowers; *A. polyphylla* has the same structure and flowering habit, but its leaves have white spots.

AGAVES

The century plant (*Agave americana*) like the aloes, grows in rosette form, but is much taller — a spiky long-lived plant, featuring elongated leaves with serrated edges. The other agave that is tough enough for outdoor life is Parry's agave (*A. parryi*), which is much shorter than *A. americana*, but just as handsome. It grows in a deep rosette-form cup shape.

Below (left, centre, right) From gravel gardens to green roofs, there are succulents to suit a wide variety of outdoor situations. Even those that won't be happy outside year-round may enjoy a garden holiday during the summer months.

PLANTING A GREEN ROOF

If you'd like to take on a succulent project outdoors, consider planting up a green roof. Originally these became popular for outdoor studios and workshops, but increasingly they're being used as 'roofs' on a much smaller scale, as covers for bin or cycle storage, so even if your garden or patio is quite small, there's often somewhere that you can fit one in. A healthy green roof looks great, even when it's only a metre or so square; not only does it allow you to indulge a taste for (even) more succulents, but you're also giving invertebrates much-needed extra habitat. Simple instructions on how to make and plant one up are easily available online — all you need is a frame to hold

the planting, a liner, planting medium and drainage, and some succulents — hardy sedums and sempervivums tend to be the most popular. And if that sounds a bit daunting to make from scratch, you can buy inexpensive kits with all the ingredients supplied. When you've finished, you've got a long-term planting that calls for very little maintenance.

FINALLY... LEAVING WELL ALONE

One last word on caring for plants out of doors. You've read up on the details and decided that, in theory at least, a plant or plants should be able to cope with life al fresco, then you've gone ahead and given it all the advantages you could — planted it in

the protection of a south-facing wall, perhaps, and ensured it's in very free-draining soil, topped with a good layer of gravel. The next step is to relax and leave it alone for a while. The carefree approach may result in the occasional casualty, but that's probably better than non-stop fretting and placing a plant under constant surveillance. Any experienced gardener — working indoors or out — will tell you that gardening's a learning process, and a plant that you worried about may surprise you by managing better than you expected.

CACTUS PROFILES

This section takes a closer look specifically at those cacti which will both make great houseplants and be relatively straightforward to care for – from the tiny *Gymnocalycium* to the impressively tall, and aptly named, blue torch cactus (*Pilosocereus pachycladus*). They're arranged in alphabetical order of their Latin names, although they're also listed under their common names in the index.

There's a mix of single- and double-page entries and some entries for species groups in cases where they have a lot of species variations that might hit the spot. They're illustrated with photographs, to show you as well as tell you how they might fit in.

BISHOP'S MITRE

Astrophytum myriostigma

As its common name implies this five-lobed cactus, a native of Chihuahua in Mexico, has a passing resemblance to a bishop's cap. The shape is appealingly strong and geometric: young plants start off round but elongate into columns as they mature. Bishop's mitre is covered with trichomes, minute clusters of very fine white hairs, which give the cactus a slightly metallic look in strong sunlight.

KEEPING BISHOP'S MITRE

This is a very popular and easily available cactus; small examples are commonly found for sale in most nurseries. It's unfussy to keep, although it does best in strong sunlight; plant it in a free-draining potting soil and put it in the brightest spot you have, year-round. During its dormancy, between September and March, it should continue to get as much light as possible but should not be watered; if it starts to look shrivelled, give it a small drink. Check it regularly for pests which may be harder to spot than usual – the trichomes on the plant look remarkably like mealybugs.

Bishop's mitre flowers in summer, when a succession of pale-yellow blooms, darker in the centre, emerge from the top of the plant.

Height: 40cm (16in)
Spread: 15cm (6in)

MONK'S HOOD CACTUS

Astrophytum ornatum

If you love the look of bishop's mitre but feel that a cactus isn't really a cactus unless it's spiky, a monk's hood cactus might be your preferred choice. It's similarly strongly shaped and lobed, but the ribs carry groups of sharp spines which are a pale yellow when they emerge but darken as they mature. It also grows much larger.

Below Spines on a monk's hood cactus change colour with age, darkening from a soft cream through a reddish yellow to brown.

KEEPING MONK'S HOOD CACTUS

Like bishop's mitre, monk's hood cactus is covered in trichomes, the tiny white hairs that reflect the light, but they tend to be more strongly marked and visible in this species. Provided that it's kept in an appropriate fast-draining potting soil, with plenty of light and warmth, it's a straightforward houseplant. Hold back on watering during the dormant period, between September and March. Encourage its potential to grow larger than other *Astrophytum* species by repotting it annually – this is best done in the late spring, at the start of its growing season, when it can be moved into a pot one size larger. The spines are very sharp, so it should be handled using cactus gloves or a newspaper collar.

Monk's hood cactus blooms in summer; its creamy-yellow scented flowers are carried at the top of the plant.

Height: 60cm (2ft)
Spread: 15cm (6in)

OLD MAN CACTUS, MONKEY CACTUS

Cephalocereus senilis

The most immediately striking feature of the old man cactus, and the one that gives it its common name, is its woolly appearance – in maturity, it can produce a crop of hair that would do credit to the Addams Family's Cousin Itt. The cactus grows in a single column which, kept indoors, may still reach as high as a metre (3ft) tall.

KEEPING OLD MAN CACTUS

Under the long, white hairs (which may turn yellowish or brown as the plant ages), old man cactus has a large number of extremely sharp grey spines, so it should always be handled using cactus gloves or a cactus collar. Kept indoors it may not flower (maturity is only reached at between 10–20 years old, and only a mature plant will flower). In its native Mexico, its columns can grow to an impressive 15 metres (50ft). Like all desert cacti, it needs an easy-draining potting soil and bright, direct light, year-round. Tail off watering in September to encourage it into a period of dormancy, and restart, sparingly, in March. Make a regular check for mealybugs, scale insect and other pests, which may conceal themselves under the hair.

Height: 1m (3ft)
Spread: 10cm (4in)

Left The luxurious silvery thatch of the old man cactus usually becomes denser as the plant matures but may gradually thin out and darken in a very old plant.

SILVER TORCH CACTUS

Cleistocactus strausii

When mature, the silver torch cactus grows in slender columns that appear to be covered with a coat of white hair, which in reality is made up of numerous very fine, white spines, giving the plant a silvery look. It's one of the faster-growing species of cacti, which can reach a good height even when kept indoors.

KEEPING SILVER TORCH CACTUS

Once mature (usually when the cactus has grown to 50cm [20in] or taller), it will flower over the summer, with large, tubular bright red flowers carried along the length of the stem. To encourage flowering, water regularly from the start of its growing season in spring, letting the potting soil dry out thoroughly before watering again. A twice-monthly feed (see p.45) may also be helpful.

Provided that it is kept dry, it can live outside during the warmer months in a sheltered spot in a garden, patio or on a balcony, but make sure that it's protected from rain showers; a cold soaking can lead to stem or root rot.

Height: 1.5m (5ft)
Spread: 8cm (3in)

Above (bottom) The trumpet-shaped red flowers of the silver torch cactus are worth waiting for: carried all down the stem, they burst through the plant's bristly coating.

CEREUS

These are columnar desert cacti that originate in arid regions of South America. They can grow very large as they age, so are best suited to a big sunny room with plenty of space to show them off. They may need slightly more attention than some other species but they're worth it: displayed singly, a *Cereus* cactus makes a very striking statement plant.

KEEPING CEREUS

Cereus need plenty of light year-round. They should be watered regularly between late spring and autumn and given a feed of liquid fertilizer twice monthly during the period of active growth in summer. Be careful to let the potting soil dry out completely before watering again, as these cacti are particularly susceptible to rot. Between October and March, while they're in dormancy, don't water at all unless you see that the stems are shrivelling slightly, in which case give the plant a small drink.

In nature, *Cereus* are pollinated by night-flying moths, so these species are night-flowering. They will flower, sometimes prolifically, when kept as houseplants, but their large, scented blooms open in the evening and close again at dawn; often the individual flowers may last only for a single night.

SPECIES TO TRY

CEREUS REPANDUS 'MONSTRUOSUS' (spiny hedge cactus or Peruvian apple cactus) – takes the spiral form of 'Spiralis' one step further: the ribs on its tall stems have noticeably wavy edges, giving it a distinctive and irregular shape. The 'apples' of its common name are edible red fruits that follow late summer flowers.

Height: 2m (6ft 6in)
Spread: 15cm (6in)

CEREUS 'SPIRALIS' (the twisted cereus)
– strongly ribbed and spiny, like *C. validus*,
but in this species the branches grow
in twisted corkscrew shapes, which give
a strikingly sculptural outline. 'Spiralis'
flowers in summer, with large pink and
white flowers that open in the evening.

Height: 1.5m (5ft)
Spread: 60cm (2ft)

CEREUS VALIDUS – has tall, spiny grey-
green stems with strongly marked ribs,
which will multiply as the plant matures.
Even when container-grown indoors, over
time it will become a sizeable plant. Blooms
in late summer; the flowers, which have
deep-pink exteriors and white centres,
open at night.

Height: 1.5m (5ft)
Spread: 10cm (4in)

RAT'S TAIL CACTUS

Disocactus flagelliformis

The rat's tail cactus is an epiphyte which lives in tropical forests, rooting itself high up on the sides of trees. It has numerous prickly ribbed stems which, hanging down, look very like the 'tails' of the plant's common name. It needs to be planted into a hanging basket or planter, in free-draining potting soil, and either hung quite high or, if it's in a planter, placed on a tall plant stand, to allow its trailing stems to hang naturally.

Below The flowers of the rat's tail cactus can vary quite widely in colour, from brilliant magenta to an orangey-red.

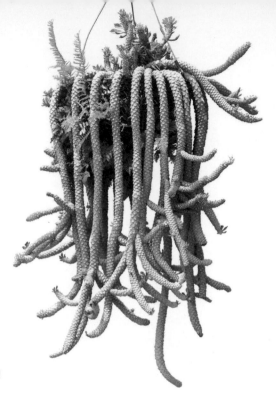

KEEPING RAT'S TAIL CACTUS

Rat's tail cactus will appreciate a degree of humidity, so will do well hung in a bathroom with indirect light, or even partial shade. If you have to hang it in a drier place, give it a daily mist with a spray bottle. Slightly cooler conditions in winter may help ensure that the plant flowers in spring, but this cactus doesn't like temperatures lower than 10°C (50°F).

Water to keep the potting soil consistently moist, but not sodden, during the growing season, and only enough to prevent the stems shrivelling during the winter. Give a twice-monthly feed of dilute liquid fertilizer during the growing season, and 'groom' regularly to keep it tidy – dead stems can simply be snipped off.

Height: Stems can trail to 90cm (3ft)
Spread: 60cm (2ft)

GOLDEN BARREL CACTUS

Echinocactus grusonii

A cactus native to central Mexico, which is small and round when young but elongates slightly as it grows until it transforms into the tubby barrel shape that matches its common name. It has strongly marked ribs studded with neatly arranged 'stars' of yellow spines along their length. The golden barrel cactus is an eye-catcher that is also reasonably easy to keep.

KEEPING GOLDEN BARREL CACTUS

This is a dry desert cactus which needs plenty of bright light. Turn it every week or two as it tends to grow toward its light source, which, unless it's countered, may spoil the plant's appealingly symmetrical shape. Plant in free-draining soil, and water sparingly during its growing season in summer, adding a dilute liquid feed once a month. Stop watering when the plant goes into dormancy, between October and March – its shallow roots can make this species especially susceptible to rot. The mature cactus will flower toward the end of summer, but the blooms are small and a rather pallid yellow; this species' main charm is the barrel shape, set off by the neat rows of spines.

Height: 50cm (20in)
Spread: 50cm (20in)

Left Golden barrel cacti grow bigger as they mature but tend not to develop additional stems.

FISHBONE CACTUS, ZIGZAG CACTUS

Epiphyllum anguliger

One look at this plant tells you where it gets its common name – the vivid green flattish stems are shaped in strong zigzags, which makes them look like rickrack braid. It's an epiphytic cactus, native to the Mexican forest, where it grows supported by the trunks and branches of trees, and as such prefers indirect light, rather than full sunlight. It will also tolerate semi-shade if necessary.

KEEPING FISHBONE CACTUS

Fishbone cactus grows upright at first, with the stems gradually dropping and hanging as they lengthen. It's best to plant it into free-draining soil in a hanging basket; it's one of the smaller epiphytic cacti, so is suitable for hanging from a lower ceiling if space is limited.

Like all epiphytes, fishbone cactus needs a fairly humid atmosphere; it should do well hung up in a bathroom, in indirect light rather than full sun. If it needs, for practical reasons, to hang somewhere drier, use a spray bottle to give it a daily misting. It should be watered regularly but left to dry out in between. Check this by putting your finger in the potting soil – if it feels dry up to the top of your first finger joint, it's ready for watering again. Skip watering altogether for a month in the middle of winter to encourage the cactus to flower later in the year. Feed with dilute liquid fertilizer twice a month in the spring and summer before it flowers in the autumn.

Flowers are a highlight: the fishbone cactus is night-flowering, so its white, sweet-scented blooms open in the evenings. Although they're short-lived, each flower lasting for only a night or two, there can be quite a number of them. The plant will sometimes go on to produce small, green fruit which are edible; enthusiasts claim they taste like gooseberries.

Height: Stems can grow to 50cm (20in)
Spread: 50cm (20in)

Left Although they're short-lived, the flowers of the fishbone cactus are very appealing; they spread a light, sweet scent when they open in the evenings.

ECHINOCEREUS

Echinocereus **species are natives of Mexico and the southern states of the US; they're all desert dwellers and they are deservedly one of the most popular groups for novices. Most make great beginner cacti – fairly small, neat, quite easy to keep, and with the bonus that many have beautiful, vibrantly coloured flowers which, in full bloom, may look almost as large as the plant itself.**

KEEPING ECHINOCEREUS

Echinocereus species aren't fussy: generally they're perfect windowsill plants which will be happy provided that they get plenty of light and aren't overwatered. They need light, free-draining potting soil and should be watered regularly – checking that the soil has dried out before watering again – for the first six months of the year. Phase out watering over autumn, and don't water at all in winter unless the plants look as though they're shrivelling slightly, indicating that they need a drink. A diluted liquid feed should be given once a month through spring and summer. Many *Echinocereus* species start with single stems, columns or spheres, but multiply to form clumps as the plants mature. Most species flower in late spring or summer.

SPECIES TO TRY

1 *ECHINOCEREUS BRANDEGEEI* (strawberry cactus/hardy hedgehog cactus) – native to the Californian desert, *E. brandegeei* has columnar stems with long, lethal-looking spines; stems may group together in a clump. Large, lilac flowers bloom along the stems in summer.

Height: 30cm (12in)
Spread: 7.5cm (3in) (individual stem)

2 *ECHINOCEREUS PENTALOPHUS* (lady finger cactus) – the 'fingers' are slender individual stems, heavily ribbed and studded with long white or yellow spines. They grow together in clumps, bearing deep pink flowers at the tips of the stems in late spring.

Height: 20cm (8in)
Spread: 20cm (8in)

3 *ECHINOCEREUS PULCHELLUS* – small, ribbed, round and spiny. The neat groups of spikes emerge from white woolly-looking areoles spaced evenly down the ribs, so the surface of the cactus appears to have a lacy pattern. Pink flowers bloom at the top of the stem in summer.

Height: 7cm (2¹/₂in)
Spread: 7cm (2¹/₂in)

3 *Echinocereus pulchellus*

4 *ECHINOCEREUS RIGIDISSIMUS* (rainbow cactus) – a pretty, deeply ribbed globe-shaped species; each year's growth of spines comes in a different shade of purple or red, giving a banded effect. Large bright pink and white flowers bloom in late spring or summer from buds that develop at the sides.

Height: 20cm (8in)
Spread: 20cm (8in) (individual globes; as it matures, the plant may form clumps)

5 *ECHINOCEREUS VIERECKII* (hedgehog cactus) – has deep-green columnar stems that grow together and are heavily ribbed and with bright yellow spines. Large, bright-pink flowers emerge in late summer.

Height: 30cm (12in)
Spread: 7.5cm (3in) (individual stem)

EMORY'S BARREL CACTUS

Ferocactus emoryi

The spines are the most immediately striking aspect of this species – they're deep red, very sharp, and can grow as long as 25cm (10in). The cactus itself is native to the desert regions in the southern states of the US and Mexico, where it can reach a height of over 2m (6ft), and even when it is kept as a houseplant, it may grow to an impressive size.

Below The ribs of this barrel cactus are lined along the whole of their length with dense spines.

KEEPING EMORY'S BARREL CACTUS

Emory's barrel cactus grows as a single stem, round when young but elongating into a barrel shape as it matures. It should be placed in full sun; make sure it's in a spot where the lethally sharp spines can do no harm and the plant can't accidentally be brushed past or pulled down. It should be planted in light, free-draining potting soil and watered carefully – like many other true desert species, this cactus is highly susceptible to stem and root rot. Water through spring and into early summer, checking the soil has thoroughly dried out before watering again, and tail off in early autumn. Only water in autumn or winter if the plant appears to be shrivelling, a sign that it's starting to dessicate; otherwise, leave it dry through its dormant period. Give a monthly dilute liquid feed in spring and summer. Flowers bloom in summer. They may be yellow, orange or red, and are sometimes followed by yellow fruit.

Height: 1m (3ft)
Spread: 40cm (16in)

DEVIL'S TONGUE CACTUS

Ferocactus latispinus

Devil's tongue cactus grows in a neat globe shape which is slate-green and heavily ribbed. Its common name comes from the unusual form of its spines: in each group of mixed white and red spines, one is larger, darker red and more curved than the others – so that it looks as though the devil is sticking his tongue out.

KEEPING DEVIL'S TONGUE CACTUS

Devil's tongue cactus grows as a single rounded stem. It originates in the arid desert of Mexico and needs light, free-draining soil and plenty of warmth and sunlight to thrive. Water in spring and summer, checking that the soil has completely dried out before watering again, then tail off in autumn and leave dry in winter unless you spot signs of withering; if you do, water once, then leave to dry out. Give a monthly dilute liquid feed in spring and summer. As with Emory's barrel cactus, you should keep this plant out of easy reach; the spikes are very sharp and there are a lot of them. When the cactus is mature it will flower in summer – the blooms are large and lilac-pink.

Height: 25cm (10in)
Spread: 25cm (10in)

Above This *Ferocactus* species really does look as though it's sticking out a myriad of little tongues.

CHIN CACTUS

Gymnocalycium bruchii

Plenty of different *Gymnocalycium* species are widely available in garden centres and nurseries, and *G. bruchii* is one of the tiniest and cutest of a group of cacti which are characteristically small and neat. If you're challenged for space, all the species in this group are worth a look. *G. bruchii* is deep green with a rounded shape and wide ribs which have groups of curved white spines along their length.

KEEPING CHIN CACTUS

Gymnocalycium species originate in South America and need plenty of bright, direct light and warmth. As with other small desert cacti, they should do well on a warm windowsill or shelf, although if they're constantly in very strong light, you may see the deep green colour become slightly bronzed by intense sun. Plant the chin cactus in light, well-draining potting soil and water regularly between March and September, allowing the soil to dry out before watering again. Give a monthly feed of diluted liquid fertilizer over the same period. Tail watering off in the autumn, giving the plant a period of dormancy until the following spring. The top of the stem is flattened, and it's here that an irregular ring of buds will develop in spring, followed by pale lilac flowers.

Height: 5cm (2in)
Spread: 6cm (2½in)

Left The spines of the chin cactus curve in a strong arch, looking like little starbursts along the plant's ribs.

BUNNY EARS CACTUS, POLKA DOT CACTUS

Opuntia microdasys

The *Opuntia* genus, or prickly pears, have round or oval pads, or cladodes, that join one another at angles; they look immediately familiar from every classic Western movie you've ever watched, and it's easy to see what prompted their common name. The bunny ears cactus is fairly easy to keep, so it's a good choice for novices.

KEEPING BUNNY EARS CACTUS

First, be careful how you handle this plant – it's covered in glochids, very fine hairs which can irritate your skin and are hard to remove, so always use gloves or a cactus collar to move it around.

The bunny ears cactus needs plenty of light, so a bright windowsill should suit it well. Plant in well-draining potting soil and water regularly during its growth period in spring and summer, making sure the soil has dried out thoroughly before watering again. Tail off watering in autumn, and leave dry in winter, unless there are signs of shrivelling, in which case water once then leave to dry out. In spring and summer, feed monthly with diluted liquid fertilizer.

When mature, this cactus will sometimes flower when kept as a houseplant but needs to be encouraged into dormancy. Keep it slightly cooler over winter, although not at temperatures below 10°C (50°F). If you succeed, the bunny ears cactus will grow pale yellow flowers from the ends of its pads.

Height: 45cm (18in)
Spread: 60cm (2ft)

Left The pads, or 'ears', give this species an appealingly characterful, almost comical look – it's an excellent choice if you like your houseplants to have personality.

MAMMILLARIA

Mostly small, easy to look after, and with lots of intriguingly different forms, *Mammillaria* cacti are an excellent group for a new enthusiast to explore. A wide range of different varieties are easily available, with a good selection stocked by many nurseries. The majority come from Mexico, although *Mammillaria* species are found scattered as widely as the southern US states, the Caribbean islands and South America.

Most of the *Mammillaria* species are either rounded in shape or form thick, short columns, and many develop clusters of stems as they mature, ultimately forming a dense mound. Within that broad picture, species are very varied: some have sharp spines, others softer bristles or hairs, in a range of colours, and the cacti themselves come in a wide variety of shades, from greyish to deep green. Like all desert species, they need free-draining potting soil and plenty of light. Water through the spring and summer, tailing off in autumn. Leave dry over the winter, and feed monthly with a diluted liquid fertilizer from March to October.

Many species will flower in late spring or summer, especially if they've had a period of dormancy; dry, and in slightly cooler temperatures over the winter months. Flowers bloom in a ring around the top of the plant.

SPECIES TO TRY

1 *MAMMILLARIA BAUMII* (pincushion cactus) – has a round, broad stem covered with soft white bristles, which has bright yellow flowers in late spring or early summer.

Height: 7.5cm (3in)
Spread: 15cm (6in) (dimensions per stem; clump-forming)

2 *MAMMILLARIA CARMENAE* (Isla Carmen pincushion cactus) – has a small, round stem covered in fountain-shaped 'explosions' of soft, pale spines which give the plant a lacy-looking surface. Pale pink flowers in late spring or early summer.

Height: 7.5cm (3in)
Spread: 10cm (4in) (dimensions per stem; clump-forming)

3 MAMMILLARIA ELONGATA (ladyfinger cactus) – one of the larger species, the ladyfinger cactus forms clusters of columnar stems which have pale pink or yellow flowers around the tops in late spring.

Height: 15cm (6in)
Spread: 5cm (2in) (dimensions per stem; clump-forming)

4 MAMMILLARIA HAHNIANA (old lady cactus) – the 'old lady' of the common name comes from the soft silver-white 'hair' that covers the round stems. It's a prolific bloomer, carrying a ring of deep-pink flowers around the stem's top from late spring.

Height: 10cm (4in)
Spread: 7.5cm (3in) (dimensions per stem; clump-forming)

5 MAMMILLARIA MAGNIMAMMA (Mexican pincushion) – one of the taller species, the Mexican pincushion's stems are covered in sharp spines. It flowers in mid-spring and sometimes again in summer; flowers range in colour from red through pink to cream.

Height: 30cm (12in)
Spread: 10cm (4in) (dimensions per stem; clump-forming)

6 MAMMILLARIA SPINOSISSIMA (spiny pincushion cactus) – has rounded but relatively tall stems. A notable feature is the double layer of spines – short and white lower on the stem; longer and orangey-red closer to the top, giving the plant an appealing bi-colour look. Flowers are small and deep pink.

Height: 30cm (12in)
Spread: 10cm (4in) (dimensions per stem; clump-forming)

MISTLETOE CACTUS, SPAGHETTI CACTUS

Rhipsalis baccifera

The mistletoe cactus is a native of the tropical rainforests of Central and South America. It's an epiphyte – that is, it grows on the sides of forest trees, and roots onto their bark for support, but it doesn't take water or nutrients from them. The plant's small white flowers, carried at the ends of the stems, are succeeded by a crop of pearlescent white berries, which give the plant its common name.

KEEPING MISTLETOE CACTUS

At first a young mistletoe cactus looks like
a shaggy, hair-like mop, but as it matures its
stems begin to trail, eventually growing to an
impressive length, so the plant will be most at
home in a hanging basket or in a pot placed on
a tall stand, from which the stems can trail as
they grow. Plant up using a commercial potting
soil or your own mix (see pp.26–27) and hang
in a room in indirect light or even partial
shade. Most epiphytic cacti enjoy the humid
atmosphere of a bathroom, but if you have
to hang yours in a room with lower humidity,
compensate by giving it a daily mist with a spray
bottle. Slightly cooler conditions in winter may
help to promote flowering in spring, but this
plant doesn't like temperatures lower than
10°C (50°F).

Water during the growing season to keep the
potting soil consistently moist, but not sodden;
during dormancy, water only occasionally –
enough to prevent the stems from shrivelling
or drying out. Give a dilute feed of suitable
fertilizer twice a month during the growing
season. If the plant starts to look untidy, rather
than appealingly dishevelled, give it a trim: dead
or disfigured stems can be simply snipped off.

Height: Trailing stems can grow to 2m (6ft 6in) in length
Spread: 60cm (24in)

Above and opposite Keep your mistletoe cactus in
the same place while it is coming into flower, otherwise
it may drop its buds, meaning that you lose both the
blooms and the berries that follow them.

GOLDEN BALL CACTUS, YELLOW TOWER CACTUS

Parodia leninghausii

The *Parodia* group of cacti make excellent houseplants; they're not fussy to look after, and they're appealingly sculptural and compact in shape. If you're looking for a plant that isn't too spiky (perhaps you have children around and only a low windowsill or shelf to put plants on) consider the golden ball cactus – its modified spines are more like soft bristles and are so numerous on some plants that it can look as though they're wearing a blond wig.

KEEPING GOLDEN BALL CACTUS

This species comes from Brazil and needs plenty of direct light and warmth. Plant it into light, well-draining potting soil and water regularly between March and September, allowing the soil to dry out before watering again. Give the plant a feed of diluted liquid fertilizer once a month over the same period. Cut back on watering in autumn, and leave the plant dry over the winter, only watering if the stem shows signs of shrivelling.

When young, the golden ball cactus grows as a single 'ball'; as it matures, the shape lengthens into a column, and it may develop other stems to form a clump. Once a golden ball cactus is mature it will bloom in the summer, with large, pale yellow, silky flowers carried at the top of the stems.

Height: 60cm (2ft)
Spread: 10cm (4in) (for a single stem)

CHRISTMAS CACTUS

Schlumbergera × buckleyi

The Christmas cactus is an epiphytic plant that originates from high-altitude rainforest in Brazil; it is probably the most familiar of all the succulents that are grown as houseplants. As an epiphyte, it appreciates more humidity than desert-dwelling cacti, and prefers semi-shade to full sun. Once its few preferences are met, it will reward you with a sensational flowering season at a time when few other plants are in bloom.

KEEPING CHRISTMAS CACTUS

Best planted in a hanging basket in free-draining potting soil, so that the green stems can trail as they grow. If you hang it in a bathroom, it will enjoy the humidity; if it needs to hang somewhere with a drier atmosphere, make sure it's in semi-shade and add some moisture by misting it daily with water from a spray. Water regularly enough to keep the potting soil slightly moist, but not wet. Give a dilute feed of suitable fertilizer twice a month between March and September.

By late autumn the fountain of deeply segmented shiny green stems will have developed buds at the tips; don't move or disturb the plant at this point, or it may drop the buds. The brilliant pink flowers will come into bloom at some point in December, hence the plant's common name.

Height: 45cm (18in)
Spread: 45cm (18in)

BLUE TORCH CACTUS

Pilosocereus pachycladus

This cactus is a native of Brazil where, growing in the wild, it can easily become the size of a small tree. Even when it's kept as a houseplant it's one of the larger options, but it is well worth the space it takes up – size, colour and appealingly sculptural shape all work together to make it a real focal point.

KEEPING BLUE TORCH CACTUS

The most immediately noticeable thing about this cactus is its colour – plenty of other species are a blueish-grey, but the blue torch is a true silvery pale blue, and very striking. The stem is deeply ribbed with tufts of wiry pale 'hair' emerging from the flattened top, and the ribs have groups of yellow spines emerging from regularly spaced areoles. As it matures, the form becomes branched, with new stems that emerge from the base of the original, central stem.

Like all desert dwellers, the blue torch cactus should be planted in free-draining potting soil and given plenty of light and warmth: the more bright sunlight it gets, the more pronounced the blue colour will become. Water regularly through spring and summer, ensuring that the soil dries out thoroughly before watering again, then tail off in autumn and leave dry in winter. Feed monthly with diluted liquid fertilizer during the growing period, between late spring and late summer.

Blue torch cacti will flower when kept as houseplants, but only when fully mature, and that's usually when the stem has grown to a metre (3ft) or more. They're night-flowerers; the flowers, which have white centres and red outer petals, are carried at the top of the stem and open in the evening.

Height: 1m (3ft)
Spread: 15cm (6in) (for a single stem)

Opposite The eye-catching blue colour and strong shape combine to make the blue torch cactus one of the best 'statement' species. Mature plants are available, at a price, if you don't want to wait for a smaller specimen to grow.

SUCCULENT PROFILES

Even when you've separated out the prickly family Cactaceae, you're left with succulents belonging to more than 50 other families, so the options are extremely varied. This section contains profiles for a lot of different sorts of plants, including some that can live outside, such as agaves; plenty of beginner-friendly choices, especially among the echeverias and stonecrops; and one or two outsize options, such as the jade plant, which can grow into very impressive container plants indeed.

As with the cacti profiles, this section is made up of a mixture of single- and double-page entries, plus a few for groups, all illustrated with photographs and clear information about plant care. Leaf through and see what catches your eye.

HOUSELEEKS

Houseleeks, or aeoniums (somewhat confusingly, sempervivums are also called 'houseleeks'), vary widely in size, with species ranging from tiny rosettes, small enough to share space in a succulent dish, to much larger shrub-like plants that will make a big impression in any room large enough to house them. Some are also tough enough to live outdoors for a lot of the year, or even year-round provided you can offer them a very sheltered spot – they won't usually survive a frost.

KEEPING HOUSELEEKS

These plants appreciate sun, but they may prefer to be kept in indirect light during a hot summer. Unlike many other succulents, their growing season runs through autumn into spring, and they can become dormant over the summer months. Like all succulents, they need a free-draining soil. They should be watered regularly between October and April, and the potting soil should be left to dry out before watering again. Give a feed of diluted liquid fertilizer once a month over the same period. Tail off the watering in late spring, watering only sparingly during the summer. Mature plants will often flower toward the end of their growing period; they are more likely to bloom if fed regularly.

SPECIES TO TRY

AEONIUM 'ZWARTKOP' (black aeonium) – like a smaller version of *A. arboreum*. Long stems hold striking shaded rosettes of leaves, deep purple at the edges and green in the centre. The vivid flowers bloom in late winter; they're bright yellow, carried in dense clusters, or panicles.

Height: 60cm (24in)
Spread: 60cm (24in)

AEONIUM ARBOREUM 'ATROPURPUREUM' (dark purple houseleek tree) – this makes a huge houseplant, with long stems and dark rosettes of burgundy-purple leaves. It flowers in spring, with upright clusters of bright yellow blooms.

Height: 1.5m (5ft)
Spread: 1.5m (5ft)

***AEONIUM HAWORTHII* 'VARIEGATUM'**
(variegated pinwheel) – mid-sized plant with
elegant rosettes of leaves which start off a pale
yellow, then deepen to green, and finally
develop pinkish-burgundy edges.

Height: 60cm (24in)
Spread: 60cm (24in)

AEONIUM CANARIENSE* VAR. *SUBPLANUM
(Canary Island flat giant houseleek) – has
unusually large rosettes, which are green in
spring and summer, but turn purple in cooler
weather. May grow yellow flower spikes from
the centres of its rosettes in spring.

Height: 50cm (20in)
Spread: 50cm (20in)

***AEONIUM* 'BLUSHING BEAUTY'** ('Blushing Beauty'
houseleek) – makes a large branched houseplant, but
with a compact habit that tends not to get too leggy, and
with notably pretty colouring. The pale green rosettes
have a subtle pinky-red 'blush' and may produce spikes
of yellow flowers in late spring.

Height 70cm (28in)
Spread 60cm (24in)

FAN ALOE

Aloe plicatilis

Aloes come in lots of shapes and sizes and the fan aloe, a native of South Africa, makes a particularly large, handsome and long-lived houseplant. Long, fleshy grey-green leaves are carried in a fan at the top of a bark-covered tree-like trunk: as the aloe grows, the lower leaves wither and are shed, and new ones grow in from the plant's centre. Mature fan aloes may develop side branches.

KEEPING FAN ALOE

Fan aloes need plenty of light and warmth, so place the plant in a bright, sunny spot, turning it every couple of weeks. Plant in free-draining potting soil and water regularly between March and October, letting the soil dry out thoroughly before watering again. Give a feed of diluted liquid fertilizer once a month over the same period. Tail off the watering in late autumn, and water only very occasionally in winter – often once a month will be enough. If you see the top leaf tips start to wither, it's usually a sign that your aloe needs a drink. Mature fan aloes kept as houseplants will often bloom, especially if they've been fed in the previous season; tall spires grow up from the centre of the leaf 'fan' and carry red, tube-shaped flowers in late spring.

Height: 1.5m (5ft)
Spread: 1m (3ft)

Left Aloes are hardy enough to enjoy some outdoor time during the warmer months provided you can offer them a sunny, sheltered location.

BARBADOS ALOE

Aloe vera

Aloe vera is a familiar ingredient in products from drinks to skin creams – to treat sunburn, simply cut a leaf from its plentiful supply (it readily grows new ones) and squeeze the soothing gel onto the skin. While this makes it a useful plant to have around, it's also good-looking and unfussy to grow, with a rosette of tall, grey-green pointed leaves with spiky edges.

KEEPING ALOE VERA

Like others in the family, this aloe needs lots of sunlight and warmth, so put it in a bright location, planted into light, free-draining potting soil and it will grow relatively fast. Water regularly between spring and early autumn, letting the soil dry out thoroughly before you water again. A container aloe should be tough enough to live outside for a month or two during a warm summer, but make sure it's in a sunny place and sheltered from any rain. Give a feed of diluted liquid fertilizer once a month over the spring and summer, and water less frequently through autumn, and only very occasionally in winter. Kept as a houseplant, *Aloe vera* doesn't usually flower.

Height: 60cm (24in)
Spread: 60cm (24in)

Below It's one of the most familiar succulents grown as a houseplant – not only is it unfussy to keep, but it provides an on-hand remedy for minor burns.

AGAVE

The *Agave* family not only includes some of the largest and most striking of all succulents, but also a number of smaller species which are well suited to growing indoors. Some, including *A. americana*, are monocarpic (meaning that they flower only once in their lives, dying after they bloom) – but they generally live long lives before they flower, hence *A. americana*'s common name: the century plant.

KEEPING AGAVES

Plant into a free-draining potting soil and site in bright light or full sun. Agaves have a period of dormancy over the winter, but they're not frost hardy; if you are growing them outside, they'll need protection from the cold and wet of winter (move pot-grown plants under cover if you can).

Make sure the planting medium has plenty of drainage added – dig in grit if you're growing an agave in open ground, and plant in free-draining potting soil if in a container. Water regularly through spring and summer, only watering again when the soil has dried out, and tail off watering in autumn as the plant enters dormancy. Keep almost dry through the winter, water only if the leaves are shrivelling. Feed monthly with diluted liquid fertilizer in spring and summer. Remove brown or withered leaves as close to the base as possible, cutting them off with a sharp knife. Agaves kept as houseplants don't usually flower.

SPECIES TO TRY

AGAVE AMERICANA (American century plant) – the biggest agave, and also the most commonly found; young plants can be grown indoors, but when mature and larger they can live outside, where they'll look good in a gravel garden or dry border. *A. americana* also has some attractive cultivars – 'Variegata' has creamy-yellow-edged leaves, and 'Mediopicta alba' has white leaves with green edges.

Height: 1.5m (5ft)
Spread: 1.5m (5ft)

AGAVE ATTENUATA (foxtail agave) – a stylish choice with smooth, wide, glaucous, spineless leaves.

Height: 1.5m (5ft)
Spread: 1.5m (5ft)

AGAVE STRICTA
(hedgehog agave) –
narrow tubular leaves
form a spiky mound,
giving this variety its
common name.

Height: 40cm (16in)
Spread: 40cm (16in)

AGAVE FILIFERA (thread
agave) – *A. filifera* forms a
compact mound of leaves
which carry white flossy
threads along their edges.

Height: 45cm (18in)
Spread: 45cm (18in)

AGAVE PARRASANA (cabbage
head agave) – wide, waxy
glaucous leaves with hooked
spines, which grow to form
a dense rosette.

Height: 60cm (24in)
Spread: 60cm (24in)

AGAVE VICTORIAE-REGINAE
(royal agave, Queen Victoria agave)
– a small plant with dark green
leaves that are edged with white and
carry sharp spines at the tips.

Height: 30cm (12in)
Spread: 60cm (24in)

AGAVE PARRYI (Parry's agave)
– pale green leaves edged and
tipped with attractive black
spines. Hardy enough to live
outdoors when mature.

Height: 50cm (20in)
Spread: 50cm (20in)

HEARTS ON A STRING

Ceropegia linearis subsp. *woodii*

One of the prettiest and most tolerant trailing succulents you can grow, hearts on a string looks exactly like its name: its delicate, heart-shaped leaves have purple undersides and variegated tops, green traced with creamy white. Leaves grow prolifically on long stems, and the plant looks wonderful in a hanging basket, or planted in a pot placed on a column, showing off the stems.

KEEPING HEARTS ON A STRING

The plant needs free-draining potting soil and plenty of sunlight. If you're planting it in a hanging basket, add perlite to make sure it's not too heavy. Water regularly in the spring and summer, allowing the soil to dry out before watering again, and give a monthly feed of diluted liquid fertilizer too. From October onward stop feeding and cut back on watering. Leave almost dry during the winter, unless you notice the leaves shrivelling slightly, in which case give the plant a drink. Hearts on a string is easy to look after and will even survive a few weeks without water if you forget about it, but if you want it to flower, try to keep up a reasonably regular water-and-feeding regime. A mature hearts on a string will produce attractive dusty-pink flowers in summer, tubular in shape with slightly swollen bases.

Height: 10cm (4in)
Length: up to 1.5m (5ft) (per stem)

Below Place or hang hearts on a string where you'll get an all-round view of the plant, so that the pretty violet-purple undersides of the leaves are visible, as well as the variegated topsides.

JADE PLANT, FRIENDSHIP TREE, MONEY PLANT

Crassula ovata

With its branching stems and rounded fleshy leaves, often tinged with red around the edges, the jade plant is a native of South Africa. It's extremely popular; justly so, since it's also good looking, long-lived and very easy to keep. It can grow impressively large (many other members of the *Crassula* group are sizeable shrubs) – if you have a big corner to fill, and limited time to cosset your plants, this is the ideal choice.

KEEPING A JADE PLANT

Jade plants prefer a free-draining light soil and should be placed in a position where they'll get plenty of sun. Water regularly between March and October, repeating only when the potting soil has had time to dry out, and feeding monthly with diluted liquid fertilizer. Stop feeding and gradually water less frequently through late autumn, then leave almost dry in winter unless you notice the leaves have begun to shrivel; if they do, give the plant a drink. Jade plants will tolerate cooler temperatures than many other succulents, provided that their roots are in dry soil; kept as houseplants, they don't usually flower, although if you move one outside for the summer, you might be rewarded with pretty small white or pink flowers. The leaves repay a regular wipe with a dry cloth; the slightly rubbery texture that is one of the appealing qualities of the plant is more noticeable when dust-free.

Above right The jade plant is both attractive and reasonably tolerant. It's a good choice if you have space for one big statement plant but tend to be a bit absent-minded with plant care.

Height: 1.5m (5ft)
Spread: 1m (3ft)

STRING OF BEADS, STRING OF PEARLS

Curio rowleyanus/Senecio rowleyanus

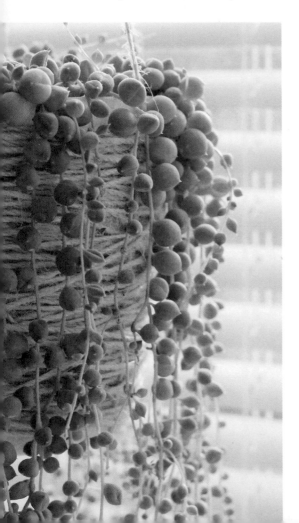

One of the most eye-catching of trailing succulents, string of pearls is a native of South Africa and Namibia. It looks exactly like its name: the rounded leaves curve in on themselves, looking like little spheres, and are spaced evenly along slender hanging stems. Show it off in a hanging basket, ideally quite high up; the plant is relatively hardy, but the stems can break easily, so it's best kept away from accidental knocks.

GROWING STRING OF PEARLS

Plant into a hanging basket, using light, free-draining soil with a proportion of perlite (if you're mixing your own, rather than using a pre-mixed commercial potting soil) to ensure that the resulting mix is not too heavy when the basket is hung. String of pearls prefers indirect light, so try to hang it somewhere bright but where it's not under direct sun.

Water regularly through spring and summer. Wait until the compost has dried out before watering again, then tail off through autumn and leave dry over winter unless you see the leaves are withering, in which case water once. Add a feed of diluted liquid fertilizer twice a year, once in April and once in July. String of pearls has small white flowers but doesn't usually produce them when it's kept as a houseplant.

Height: 10cm (4in)
Length: up to 1m (3ft) (per stem)

Left The stems of string of pearls are easily broken, but a healthy plant regenerates quickly, producing literally dozens of 'strings' over a season.

PINCUSHION EUPHORBIA

Euphorbia enopla

At first glance you might mistake this member of the extensive *Euphorbia* group for a cactus; a second will show you that the plant doesn't have areoles. Keep well out of the way of pets and children, and use gloves to handle it – not only are the ribbed stems studded with formidably long red spines, but if damaged, the white sap that oozes out can be a skin irritant.

KEEPING PINCUSHION EUPHORBIA

In its natural habitat, the drylands of South Africa, the pincushion euphorbia can grow to heights of over a metre (3ft), but kept as a container plant, it's unlikely to reach more than 60cm (24in) and as a slow grower it may take years to get there.

Plant into light, well-draining potting soil and keep it in as bright and warm a location as you can offer. Water regularly between March and October, allowing the compost to dry out before watering again. A monthly feed of diluted liquid fertilizer can be added. Tail off watering through autumn and leave the plant dry in winter; if the stems start to look shrivelled, water once. Kept as a houseplant, the pincushion euphorbia may bloom in summer with small red or yellow flowers, carried at the top of the stems.

Height: 60cm (24in)
Spread: 40cm (16in)

Above right The pincushion euphorbia looks striking in a mixed succulent planter – use less aggressively prickly plants around it to provide contrast and protect your hands.

ECHEVERIA

Echeverias are natives of South and Central America, up to the southern US. They grow in rosettes and most are quite small; within that broad definition, there are numerous variations of form and colour. Don't allow yourself to be confused by the common names: a lot of different species go under the 'hen and chicks' label. If you spot one you like the look of online or in someone else's collection, check the Latin name too, so you can be sure what it is.

KEEPING ECHEVERIAS

These are great plants for novices: they're generally easygoing and can cope with slightly lower temperatures than some other succulents. Plant into light, free-draining potting soil and position somewhere sunny; most species are hardy enough to be kept outdoors in a sheltered spot during the summer months. Water regularly through spring and summer, their growing season, and give a monthly feed of dilute liquid fertilizer. Wait until the soil dries out before watering again and reduce from September onward. Allow to dry out completely during winter, only watering if the leaves start to look desiccated. Many species will flower in summer; long, narrow stems emerge from the rosettes, with the flowers blooming on the ends.

SPECIES TO TRY
....

ECHEVERIA LEUCOTRICHA (chenille plant) – reflecting the name, the rosettes of this species are covered with grey, velvety down. In summer the plant produces spires of orange flowers.

Height: 15cm (6in)
Spread: 25cm (10in)

ECHEVERIA AGAVOIDES 'TAURUS'
(moulded wax 'Taurus') – one of the
larger species, featuring striking large
purple-red rosettes and, in summer,
red flowers.

Height: 15cm (6in)
Spread: 30cm (12in)

ECHEVERIA ELEGANS (Mexican snow
ball) – as elegant as its name, fleshy
rosettes in a pale blue-grey, with arching
stems of pink flowers in late spring.

Height: 10cm (4in)
Spread: 20cm (8in)

ECHEVERIA AMOENA (hen and chicks) – the
swollen grey-green leaves of this tiny species,
sometimes reddish at the edges, look a little
like jelly beans. Red stems grow from the
rosettes in late spring, carrying long-lived
coral-coloured flowers.

Height: 2.5cm (1in)
Spread: 5cm (2in)

ECHEVERIA LAUI (hen and chicks) – striking
species whose fat blue-grey leaves have a
powdery look; chunky stems emerge from
the rosettes in summer, carrying bright
pink and orange flowers.

Height: 10cm (4in)
Spread: 20cm (8in)

OX TONGUE PLANT

Gasteria brachyphylla

A compact species, originating from South Africa, the ox tongue plant has an interesting structure with wide strap-shaped leaves that grow alternately on each side of a single stem, resulting in a neat sculptural shape that looks a little like a fan. The leaves are mottled with a banded pattern made up of fine white spots. In summer, mature plants will grow tall stems which carry pink flowers.

KEEPING AN OX TONGUE PLANT

This is one of the faster-growing succulents. It is happiest in indirect light; find it a bright spot but out of direct sunlight – in the wild, it tends to grow slightly shaded by taller plants. Plant in light, free-draining potting soil and water regularly between March and September, ox tongue plant's growing season. Feed it only once a year, in spring, with dilute liquid fertilizer. Wait until the soil has dried out before watering again, and gradually cut back on watering from September onward. Allow to dry out completely during winter, only giving it a drink if the leaves start to look shrivelled.

Height: 25cm (10in)
Spread: 20cm (8in)

Below The neat fan structure, with leaves symmetrically arranged, means the ox tongue is easily recognized, and earns it a place in a line-up of sculptural plants.

SWEETHEART PLANT

Hoya kerrii

The sweetheart plant is a vigorous epiphytic climber, a native of Southeast Asia which is named for its fleshy heart-shaped leaves. When mature and even when it's being kept as a container houseplant, it can grow – quickly – to a considerable size. Single-leaf cuttings are widely sold as cute, heart-shaped gifts, but if you want to grow it, it's better to find a small plant; while even the small cuttings will usually produce shoots eventually, a plant will grow enthusiastically straight away.

KEEPING A SWEETHEART PLANT
It's a climbing vine rather than a trailer, so you need to give a sweetheart plant something to climb. As an epiphyte, it prefers a humid atmosphere and indirect light – a situation growing up the side of a bathroom window, for example, will suit it very well. Plant it into free-draining potting soil and water regularly through spring and summer, leaving the soil to dry out before watering again. Tail watering off from September and water only occasionally for the rest of the year. If the plant is growing in a drier atmosphere – a centrally heated living room, say – mist it daily with a spray to give it a bit more humidity. Feed monthly during the growing season with diluted liquid fertilizer. In summer it carries heads of white flowers with deep pink centres.

Height: 4m (13ft)
Spread: 1m (3ft)

Above and right A single sweetheart leaf cutting looks appealing, but if you want faster results, opt for a full plant, complete with stem, like the one on the right.

DWARF KALANCHOE

Kalanchoe pumila

The dwarf kalanchoe is a delicate and pretty plant which is native to Madagascar. It grows into a small bush shape, and both leaves and flowers are attractive. The leaves have serrated edges and are covered in extremely fine silvery hairs, which give them a matt finish, as though they have been lightly powdered, and the pink, lilac-lined flowers are carried in clusters on fragile grey stems.

KEEPING DWARF KALANCHOE

Plant in light, well-draining potting soil and keep in a bright location with indirect light. Kalanchoes need watering according to the season: in spring, allow the soil to dry out thoroughly before watering again; in summer, water enough for the soil to stay slightly moist to the touch (it shouldn't, however, feel wet); in autumn, once again allow it to dry out thoroughly before watering again, and in winter, water only very occasionally if the leaves show signs of starting to shrivel. Feed monthly between April and September with a diluted liquid fertilizer.

In nature, dwarf kalanchoe will flower in late winter to early spring, but the timing can be less predictable when it is being kept as a houseplant. After it has flowered (even if it wasn't when you expected) the plant needs a clear period of dormancy to flower again the following year, so when flowering is over, trim off the dead stems, and move the kalanchoe to a shaded corner for six weeks, checking it weekly and watering only if the leaves start to wither. Put it back in its usual spot when the six weeks is up.

Height: 30cm (12in)
Spread: 30cm (12in)

Below The grey and lilac colouring and delicate shape of the dwarf kalanchoe makes it a distinctive addition to a succulent line-up.

LIVING STONES

Lithops

Native to stony regions of southern Africa, living stones look exactly as they sound, mimicking small rocks or stones with almost uncanny effectiveness. There are a number of different species, but all consist of two fat leaves, with almost no stem, the pair divided only by a shallow channel, in mottled colours and patterns that range from dull greens to stony greys and browns. In the wild, this camouflage allows them to avoid the attentions of grazing animals.

KEEPING LIVING STONES

Living stones need full sun; a bright windowsill is the ideal position for them. They should be planted in free-draining potting soil with an additional helping of grit; a gravel top dressing will show them off nicely. New growth appears in late winter when the existing leaves start to wither away and a fresh pair pushes out between them. The new plant will produce flowers that look rather like dandelions in late summer or autumn and, after flowering, will start to wither in its turn as the cycle repeats

itself. Between March and September water regularly, waiting until the soil has dried out before watering again. Stop watering after the plant has flowered and leave it to dry out until the end of winter, when the new growth becomes visible once again. Give a single feed of diluted liquid fertilizer in spring, as the new leaves come into growth.

Height: 4cm (1 1/2in)
Spread: 8cm (3in)

Above right The huge range of colours and subtle patterns of living stones can make them addictive to collect: you can display a wide variety in a single medium-sized planter.

SEDUMS

Sedums, or stonecrops, are some of the most familiar and appealing species for a new succulent enthusiast. They're a big group and many are robust enough to live outside for at least part of the year. They can often be identified by their characteristically fleshy 'jelly bean' leaves, but they come in a range of sizes, too, so whatever space you have available, inside or out, you should be able to find a species to suit.

Plant into free-draining potting soil and position in a bright, sunny spot. Water regularly between March and September, waiting for the soil to dry out before watering again. Feed monthly over the same period, using a diluted solution of liquid fertilizer. Reduce watering from September onward, and tail it off through winter, watering only enough to prevent the leaves from withering. You can move them outside during the summer months, but make sure the plants are sheltered from rain, as the roots will rot if they sit in wet soil for any length of time.

SPECIES TO TRY

SEDUM × RUBROTINCTUM (banana cactus, jelly bean plant) – named for their shape, rather than their slatey-green colour, swollen curving leaves with red tips grow in spirals around the stems. Produces yellow flowers in summer.

Height: 20cm (8in)
Spread: 20cm (8in)

SEDUM MORGANIANUM (donkey's tail, burro's tail) – trailing strings of plump leaves tip over the side of the pot and fall down in 'tails', the tips of which produce deep pink flowers in summer.

Height: 1cm (4in)
Spread: 30cm (12in)

SEDUM PACHYPHYLLUM (blue jelly bean) – a fast-growing, sprawling species, with pretty, loose stems of fat blue-green 'jelly bean' leaves and bright yellow flowers in summer.

Height: 25cm (10in)
Spread: 25cm (10in)

SEDUM NUSSBAUMERIANUM (coppertone stonecrop) – as the name implies, the chunky green leaves of this variety have coppery tints around their edges. The plant has small, white, star-shaped flowers in summer.

Height: 15cm (6in)
Spread: 20cm (8in)

COBWEB HOUSELEEK

Sempervivum arachnoideum

The cobweb houseleek is one of the most picturesque members of an attractive family. Sempervivums, also known as houseleeks (as are aeoniums – see pp.108–109), are small plants which grow in rosettes; they're fairly hardy, and they're straightforward to look after. Cobweb houseleeks stand out from other species because they have what looks like a spider's web, a delicate nest of woolly threads, spun around the rosette; this species is also particularly quick to produce offsets (new small plants clustering around the parent rosette – see p.133), so you also get the side benefit of free plants.

KEEPING COBWEB HOUSELEEK

Houseleeks like free-draining potting soil and plenty of sun, so place on a bright windowsill or outside in a sunny sheltered corner during the warmer months. When plants are outside, make sure they can drain freely after rain showers, as the roots will rot if they're left sitting in water for any length of time. Indoors, water regularly between March and September but wait for the soil to dry out before watering again. Feed monthly over the same period, using a diluted solution of liquid fertilizer. Gradually reduce the frequency of watering from September onward, and tail it off through winter, watering only if you see that the leaves are starting to wither.

In summer, strong stems emerge from the rosettes of the houseleek, carrying flat clusters of small, starry pink flowers. If you like this species, there are a couple of other varieties that may interest you: cobweb houseleek 'Rubrum' (*Sempervivum arachnoideum* 'Rubrum') has the same weblike covering, but with rosettes that are mostly purplish-red, while the moss-like cobweb houseleek (*Sempervivum arachnoideum* var. *bryoides*) is a kind of doll's-house version with cutely minute rosettes that measure barely a centimetre across.

Height: 10cm (4in)
Spread: 10cm (4in)

Right Don't be misled – although the geometrical webbing around the tops of cobweb houseleek stems can look remarkably like a spider's web, the plant produces it naturally.

CHAPTER FIVE

Creating New Plants

One of the great pleasures of collecting succulents is how easy it is to grow new plants from the ones you've got. Quite a few species produce them with absolutely no input from the gardener; all you have to do is delicately scoop the infants out of the original pot, removing them from their parents and setting them up on their own. Other new plants can be grown from leaf and stem cuttings – not difficult techniques to master – or, in the cases of many cacti and some other succulents, from seed.

This short chapter looks at the different ways to grow new plants, and at which method is likely to suit which group of plants the best. If you grow your own, you'll find that not only is it a good way to increase the numbers of your plants, but you'll also be creating a constant source of swaps that you can make with other succulent enthusiasts to widen the number of different species in your own collection.

GROWING FROM SEED AND TAKING OFFSETS

Because cacti and succulents tend to be seen as specialist plants you may not have thought of growing them from seed in the same way that you might grow, say, cosmos or carrots, but provided that you can get your hands on the right seeds they're no more difficult to grow than other kinds of plant. Taking offsets is even easier – new plants with an absolute minimum of effort.

WHERE TO FIND SEEDS

Online, you'll find plenty of seeds for sale, both on general plant sales sites and on sites that are specialists in succulents and cacti. The range may include packets of seeds for specific species, or sometimes for groups of plants – you might see a packet of mixed seeds for *Mammillaria* species, for example – or, occasionally, they may be labelled even more generically – 'Mixed cacti seeds', for instance (perhaps one to go for if you like a surprise…).

Regular nurseries or DIY/gardening stores may have a few packets of seed for sale, but the choice is generally quite limited. Finally, you will sometimes find seeds if you visit a specialist succulent nursery, where they will have been collected from their own plants. If you opt for the last option, ask about the best way to germinate seeds and raise young plants while you're there; they may have useful knowledge to share.

GROWING FROM SEED

Sowing is best done in spring, to give the seedlings a good start during the warmer months of late spring and summer. To start the seeds off, fill some small plastic pots, no bigger than 10cm (4in) diameter, with regular peat-free potting soil mixed in with plenty of grit. Place them in a tray of water and leave for half an hour or so, by which time the top surface of the soil will be moist.

Take the pots out of the tray and sprinkle the seeds thinly over the top of the soil in the pots. Check the packet for any specific instructions – some seeds may need a very light covering of soil over them, while others may be better left on the surface, for example – and also check how long it usually takes for the seeds to germinate. Even the faster species may take a month or two; occasionally germination can take more than six months, so do check on what you can expect for the particular species you're planting.

Label the pots with the species and the date they were sown, then place each pot in a clear plastic bag and leave somewhere with indirect light (don't leave them in full sun). Tuck the top of each bag under the pot to give it its own miniature greenhouse. In the days that follow, take each pot out of its bag every day for an hour to ensure condensation doesn't build up too much.

Above left How long succulent seeds take to germinate varies widely, depending not only on species, but also on the ambient temperature around them and when you sow them. These *Aloe vera* seeds took less than a month to sprout.

FROM SEEDLINGS TO SMALL PLANTS

When the seeds germinate, remove the plastic bag altogether and leave the pots with their new seedlings somewhere bright but, again, not in direct light, to grow. Check the moisture of the soil every couple of days – it shouldn't be wet, but if it feels very dry, give it a couple of spritzes with water from a spray bottle; very young seedlings can't be left to dry out altogether.

It may take six or eight months before the new seedlings are big enough to be potted up singly; when they're large enough to extract, use a pointed teaspoon or tweezers to gently loosen the earth around them, then spoon each one out, and put it into an individual small pot. Use a spray bottle to moisten them every few days (the soil should feel very slightly moist if you push the top joint of your finger into the pot). Once they are between 1cm (½in) and 2.5cm (1in) tall, you can start to water and care for them as you would adult plants of the same species.

SUCCULENT BABIES

If you have enough room to house your baby succulents, growing from seed is the easiest way to generate lots of new plants – useful if you have space to fill, or if you want extras for swaps with other gardeners.

TAKING OFFSETS
....

Once you've got the beginnings of a collection, you'll notice quite quickly that some types of plants are producing additional 'baby' stems or rosettes alongside the main 'parent'. These offsets, or 'pups', can be separated and potted up on their own to make new plants.

Have a pot ready, planted up with a free-draining mixture with plenty of grit, and use tweezers or a teaspoon to dig around one of the offsets and gently tease it away from the parent plant. Go under the offset to ensure that you don't separate the stem from its roots, and remove it whole, then plant it up in its new home and place it in indirect light or even semi-shade. Water once, then leave to dry out before watering again.

Groups that usually produce offsets include agaves, aloes, echinocereus, mammillarias and parodias. They're also commonly found in echeverias and sempervivums.

GROWING NEW PLANTS FROM LEAF AND STEM CUTTINGS

Cuttings are a straightforward way to propagate many species of succulent. Generally, if the leaves are very fleshy, a leaf cutting will 'take' and make a new plant. You can take stem cuttings from some other species, notably the ones with woodier stems. Finally, when the tall stems of cacti sustain damage, you can sometimes stage an emergency rescue – and end up with a new plant.

Crassula ovata

GROWING FROM A LEAF CUTTING

The best time to take a leaf cutting is in spring – the plant will have emerged from dormancy and be entering a period of growth, and temperatures are usually slightly higher (cold can make the whole propagation process slower). To start, you need to cut a leaf off cleanly, using a sharp knife, so that the end is neat and not ragged. Choose a leaf from the freshest growth, rather than an older one from the base of the plant.

Line a plate or tray with a few sheets of kitchen towel. Lay the leaf on them and leave the plate somewhere dry and warm, but not under bright light. The wound where it was cut needs to develop a callus, like a scab, before the leaf can start to grow its own root system and make a new plant. The callus will stop the new plant taking in too much water while the roots and leaves form. The process can be quite slow – it usually takes at least two weeks, and sometimes much longer. Make sure the leaf stays dry, as it can easily rot at this stage if it gets wet.

WHICH GROUPS SUIT LEAF CUTTINGS?

Check the Latin name for any succulent you want to take a leaf cutting from. It's usually straightforward with plants from the following groups: *Crassula*, *Echeveria*, *Kalanchoe* (which can also be propagated from stem cuttings), *Opuntia* and *Sedum*.

Opuntia

Check the leaf cutting regularly and when the cut area looks as though it's made a 'skin', it's ready to go in a pot. Some leaves will already have started to make roots by the time they have callused, but whether or not that's the case, once the callus has formed the leaf can be planted up. Fill a small pot – no bigger than 7.5cm (3in) diameter – with peat-free soil mixed with plenty of grit to ensure it drains freely. Very gently push the callused end of the leaf into the soil surface. If it has already started to produce roots, make sure that they're covered.

Water lightly, repeating every few days – the surface of the soil should feel very slightly damp. As the roots take and small shoots start to appear, the original leaf will start to shrivel. Once the cutting has definitely 'taken' and you can see a small plant growing, you can simply pull the withered old leaf away – gently – and you'll be left with a fresh new plant.

Above Wait until the old leaf pulls away easily before removing it, or you may disturb the roots of the new plant.

GROWING FROM A STEM CUTTING

The process for taking a stem cutting is similar to that for taking a leaf cutting but if anything even simpler. Cut a side shoot, ideally at least 7.5cm (3in) long, from a suitable species, take off any lower leaves, sparing just the top ones, and leave on a plate lined with paper towel in a warm, dry place until the cut end of the stem has callused over. Then repeat the same process for potting up and watering as you would with a leaf cutting.

Kalanchoe

WHICH GROUPS SUIT STEM CUTTINGS?

Check the Latin name of the plant if you want to take a stem cutting. It's usually straightforward with plants from the following groups: *Aeonium*, *Cereus*, *Cleistocactus*, *Euphorbia* and *Hoya*. *Kalanchoe* plants will usually propagate successfully from either a leaf or a stem cutting.

Epiphytes such as *Epiphyllum*, *Rhipsalis* and *Schlumbergera* will easily take from stem cuttings, too.

Hoya

EMERGENCY SURGERY

Sometimes the stem of a cactus seems to collapse from the base or near the middle without it seeming to immediately affect the top of the stem. If this proves to be full-on rot there may not be very much you can do, but you can sometimes salvage the stem by treating the top part as though you were taking a stem cutting – cut it off at least 2.5cm (1in) away from any problem, leave it in a dry, warm place to callus and, once callused, plant it up.

GLOSSARY

AREOLE
A small, raised bump found on the surface of a cactus plant, from which spines and flowers grow.

CACTUS
A family of plants that falls within the larger categorization of succulents. Cacti are native to the Americas and, unlike other succulents, have areoles.

CALLUS
The 'skin' that needs to grow over the cut end of a leaf or stem cutting before it can successfully be planted.

CLADODE
A flattened stem that doesn't develop leaves, such as, for example, the flattened 'pads' of a bunny ears cactus (see p.97).

DORMANCY
A period of time during which a plant is inactive, with reduced photosynthesis, in between periods of active growth.

EPIPHYTE
Non-parasitic plant that lives on other plants. Epiphytic cacti, which live on trees in tropical climates, are sometimes also known as 'tropical' or 'orchid' cacti.

GLAUCOUS
Usually applied to foliage; a grey-green colour often with a powdery finish or bloom.

GLOCHID
Very fine barbed fibre produced from the areoles of some cacti, mostly belonging to the prickly pear (*Opuntia*) group. Glochids irritate the skin; it's best to wear gloves to handle any plants that produce them.

HORTICULTURAL GRIT

Coarse grit which is added to the potting soil in which succulents are planted in order to improve its drainage.

MONOCARPIC

A plant which flowers only once in its lifetime, dying after flowering is completed.

OFFSET

A small plant, grown by means of an underground runner, which grows alongside the parent plant.

PANICLE

A loose cluster of flowers, held along a stem.

PERLITE

A white mineral material made by heating volcanic glass until it 'pops' into small granules that look like little pieces of polystyrene. It's used to improve the drainage of potting soil and to lighten it overall.

PUP

Alternative name for an offset; a young plant produced by means of a runner from a parent plant.

SPINE

A sharp, needle-like modified leaf, created to dissuade grazing animals from eating the plants that carry them.

STOMATE

Small holes that are the 'pores' of a leaf, allowing gas to enter or leave a plant, and which are necessary for photosynthesis.

SUCCULENT

A large group of plants, with members in up to 60 different families, that are categorized together because of shared characteristics, in particular their fleshy stems and leaves, in which they can store water as a protection against drought.

TERRARIUM

A glass container like a tank, which may be either open or closed, used to grow small plants. Most succulents need to be planted in the open type if they are to thrive in a terrarium, or the accumulated humidity will cause them to rot.

TOP DRESSING

A layer of small stones or pebbles used to dress the top surface of a plant's container; it has several uses – to improve drainage after watering, to suppress any weeds from growing and to give a neat finish.

VARIEGATED

Leaves which have variations and patterns in different colours, rather than being a single colour overall.

FURTHER RESOURCES

Make the Royal Horticultural Society (RHS) website your first port of call – it offers a mass of free information about cacti and succulents and dozens of sources where you can buy plants, both in person and online. You can find it at www.rhs.org.uk

BOOKS

Garden Succulents: Royal Horticultural Society Wisley Handbook
Terry Hewitt
(Cassell, 2003)

The Kew Gardener's Companion to Growing Houseplants
Kay Maguire
(White Lion Publishing, 2019)

RHS Practical Cactus and Succulent Book: How to Choose, Nurture and Display 200 Cacti and Succulents
Fran Bailey and Zia Allaway
(Dorling Kindersley, 2019)

RHS Practical Houseplant Book
Fran Bailey and Zia Allaway
(Dorling Kindersley, 2018)

Prick: Cacti and Succulents, Choosing, Styling, Caring
Gynelle Leon
(Mitchell Beazley, 2017)

Tiny Plants
Leslie F. Halleck
(Cool Springs Press, 2021)

USEFUL WEBSITES

British Cactus and Succulent Society
society.bcss.org.uk
Extensive and engrossing site for succulent
enthusiasts – less easy to navigate than some
others, but with masses of useful information
once you've learned to make your way around it.

Crafty Plants
craftyplants.co.uk
Online sales only, based in the north-west
of England. Specialists in *Tillandsia* (air plants),
but with good smallish sections of cacti and
succulents; also offers mixed groups of
succulents at competitive prices.

Craig House Cacti
craighousecacti.co.uk
Specialist and award-winning growers, with a
range of mail-order seeds available.

Hortology
hortology.co.uk
Extensive and popular online site for houseplants,
with a large section of cacti and succulents.

Ottershaw Cacti
ottershawcacti.com
RHS Gold medal-winning growers' nursery
based in Chertsey. Interesting selection of
plants by mail order, and plenty of information
on the website. Nursery can be visited by
appointment only.

RHS Plants
rhsplants.co.uk
The RHS's own mail order plant site. Both
individual cacti and small collections of species
are available.

Succulent Plants UK
succulentplants.uk
Online-only sales with an interesting selection,
ranging from quite large plants to inexpensive
DIY leaf or stem cuttings which you can buy to
grow on to the next stage. Includes a blog and a
lot of useful information on individual species.

Surreal Succulents
surrealsucculents.co.uk
Site that looks at planting and design ideas
for succulents, as well as the plants themselves.
Sells a range of plants and accessories, including
terrariums and kits. Includes sections on care
and FAQs.

INDEX

CREDITS

Alamy 17br © Graham Turner • 26 © Mint Images Limited • 64 © David Humphreys • 87r © Dorling Kindersley ltd • 91 © Dorling Kindersley ltd • 93br © Florapix • 109cl © Stephan Dagobert von Mikusch-Buchberg • 109cr © adrian davies • 118b © blickwinkel • 125tl © Dorling Kindersley ltd

Creative Commons 15b CC BY-ND 2.0 | ClatieK • 49t CC BY-ND 3.0 | PassionAndTheCamera • 93tl CC-BY-SA | Colin Bundred | LLIFLE www.llifle.com • 118t CC BY-SA 3.0 | RI

Dreamstime 68t © Soniabonet • 95 © Patcharamai Vutipapornkul • 105t © Marina Volkova • 105b © Miriam Doerr

Getty Images 32 © Thomas Barwick • 62 © Westend61 • 74 © Kilito Chan

iStock 33 © Hiraman • 68b © IKvyatkovskaya

Pixabay 83 © PublicDomainPictures | 17902 images

Shutterstock 5tl © Marinesea • 5tr © panattar • 5cl © denise1203 • 5cr © TYNZA • 5bl © aquaru • 5br © Anna Mente • 6 © jeep2499 • 7t © HelloRF Zcool • 7b © SUPREEYA-ANON • 10 © Shadow Inspiration • 12 © Davdeka • 13l & 13r © Scisetti Alfio • 14 © KarenHBlack • 15t © Rastislav Jarunek • 15c © Dewin ID • 16t © TRL • 16cl © pundapanda • 16cr © optimarc • 16b © Kabardins photo • 17tl © WITSALUN • 17tr © komuna photo • 17ct © Dmitrij Skorobogatov • 17cb © andregric • 17bl © Tomas Ragina • 18 © Followtheflow • 19tl & 19tr © mokjc • 19b © korkeng • 20 © artpritsadee • 21 © Africa Studio • 23tl © Followtheflow • 23tr © Inna Reznik • 23b © Akkalak Aiempradit • 24 © Soundsnaps • 25 © areetham • 27 © naramit • 28 © Sasapin Kanka • 29 © Tarda Santo • 30 © Vera Prokhorova • 34 © Eric Surprenant • 35t © Videowokart • 35ct © ANUCHA PALAMA • 35c © merrymuuu • 35cb © Dewin ID • 35b © Christina Siow • 36 © Artman96 • 37t © Maritxu • 37b © Konstantin Aksenov • 38 © Maytrobus • 39l © VasylMartynenko • 39r © New Africa • 41 © Mlle Sonyah • 42 © AjayTvm • 43 © Vladimir Sidorov69 • 44 © sattahipbeach • 45 © Olga Perm • 46 © wat hiran • 47 © Bogdan Sonjachnyj •

48 © panattar • 49ct © KsenQO • 49cb © khlungcenter • 49b © FlySakura • 50t © Anna K Mueller • 50b © Ashley-Belle Burns • 54 © Kipiani Alex • 56 © Roselynne • 57 © panattar • 60 © Alice Rodnova • 61t © JIANG HONGYAN • 61c © ShalenaOlena • 61b © Creative Vyas • 65t © Diana Taliun • 65c © InfoFlowersPlants • 65b © Sarah2 • 66 © Jantanee Boonkhaw • 67t © aapsky • 67b © Anastasia Gubinskaya • 70 © Daria Minaeva • 71 © Try_my_best • 72 © artpritsadee • 75 © Marinesea • 76 © REN Photography • 77t © Rachasie • 77b © asharkyu • 78l © anystock • 78–79c © Ellyy • 79r © Deniza 40x • 81 © Zhuravleva Katia • 82 © Abc_u • 84 © NamFang • 85t © CoinUp • 85b © Galumphing Galah • 86 © Miriam Doerr Martin Frommmherz • 87l © Thanu Garapakdee & AleksMaks • 88t © Hao_Stocker • 88b © BlackFarm • 89b © Parichart Thummarati • 90 © Lili Aini • 93tr © GracePhotos • 93bl © Cola Lemon • 94 © Besjunior • 96 © AdaCo • 97 © Phawat • 98t © COULANGES • 98b © Kwansuda Carnabuci • 99tl © Yetkin BILGIN • 99tr © uventa6 • 99bl © Sirinya_l • 99br © AP focus • 100 © nnattalli • 101t © Gaia Conventi • 101b © Martino77 • 102 © Panrinya panplang • 103 © Madlen • 104 © kikpokemon • 107 © New Africa • 108 © Natalya Yudina • 109t © Millward Shoults • 109b © mizy • 110 © John Dvorak • 111l © wasanajai • 111r © Tanya NZ • 112 © AkwaN • 113tl © PRILL • 113tr © Flash Vector • 113cl, 113cr & 113bl © Aniroot Mankhamnert • 113br © RUNGSAN NANTAPHUM • 114 © Job Narinnate • 115 © DK_2020 • 116 © MariaNikiforova • 117 © RF97 • 119t © NatVV • 119c © TYNZA • 119b © COULANGES • 120 © Christina Siow • 121t © Maryana Volkova • 121b © Irina Borsuchenko • 122 © Estudios Miguel • 123 © Pavaphon Supanantananont • 124 © panattar • 1 25tr © Maryana Volkova • 125b © Yen- ting • 126 © Carminha_B • 127t © Luoxi • 127b © Fern Farm Plants • 128 © denise1203 • 130 © chakkraphong jinthawet • 131l © finchfocus • 131r © Photology1971 • 132 © Nwxterra • 133t & 133c © Christina Siow • 133b © Aninka Bongers-Sutherland • 134 © whitemaple • 135t © Andrey_Nikitin • 135b © schab • 136 © Aninka Bongers-Sutherland • 137t © aniana • 137c © haya.pictura • 137b © kampol Jongmeesuk • 138 © LunaKate • 140 © M Kunz • 141 © helshik.